Bathroom Design

Jane Moss Snow

National Association of Home Builders
15th and M Streets NW
Washington, DC 20005

Bathroom Design

ISBN 0-86718-296-2
Library of Congress Catalog Card Number 87-61988

When ordering this publication, please provide the following information:

Title
ISBN 0-86718-296-2
Price
Quantity
NAHB membership number (as it appears on the *Builder* or *Nation's Building News* label)
Mailing address (including street number and zip code)

Cover photo was provided by Owens Corning   9/87 SCOTT/SS

Acknowledgments

Bathroom Design was produced under the general direction of Kent Colton, NAHB Executive Vice President, and by the following NAHB staff members: James E. Johnson, Staff Vice President, Information Services; Denise L. Darling, Staff Vice President, Publishing Services; Susan D. Bradford, Publications Director; Ann Elizabeth Gilmore, Editor; and David Rhodes, Art Director. Martin Mintz, NAHB Director of Technical Services and Donald Carr, of Legacy Homes, served as technical reviewers. Timothy P. Fennell provided drawings for the book.

Special thanks are due to American Standard for contributing computer-assisted design drawings to the book. In addition, the following organizations provided the photographs:

Amerec Corporation
P.O. Box 3825-T
Bellvue, WA 98009

American Standard, Inc.
40 W. 40th Street
New York, NY 10081

Armstrong World Industries, Inc.
P.O. Box 3001
Lancaster, PA 17604

Artistic Brass
4100 Ardmore Avenue
South Gate, CA 90280

Avonite®, Inc.
12836 Arroyo Street
Sylmar, CA 91432

Broan Manufacturing Company, Inc.
Hartford, WI 53027

Color Design Art
17315 Sunset Boulevard
Pacific Palisades, CA 90272

Dornbracht
Santile International Corporation
1201 West Loop North
Houston, TX 77055

DuPont Co.
Wilmington, DE 91432

Formica Corporation
1501 Broadway, Suite 1519
New York, NY 10036

Jacuzzi Inc.
11511 New Benton Hwy.
Little Rock, AR 72209

Kaufman Meeks, Inc.
14455 Grisby
Houston, TX 77079

Kohler Company
Kohler, WI 53044

Nevamar® Corporation
8339-T Telegraph Road
Odenton, MD 21113

Owens Corning Fiberglas Corporation
Fiberglas Tower
Toledo, OH 43659

Poggenpohl
6 Pearl Court
Allendale, NJ 07410

St. Charles Manufacturing Co.
1611 East Main Street
St. Charles, IL 60174

Tile Council of America, Inc.
P.O. Box 326
Princeton, NJ 08542

Villeroy & Boch
Interstate 80 at New Maple Avenue
Pine Brook, NJ 07058

Wenczel Tile Co.
200 Enterprise Avenue
P.O. Box 5308
Trenton, NJ 08638

West and Associates, Architects
2606 Perimeter Center East
Atlanta, GA 30346

Whirlpool Corporation
6300 S. Syracuse, Suite 700
Englewood, CO 80111

Wilsonart Laminated Plastics Company
600 General Bruce Drive
Temple, TX 76501

Wood-Mode Cabinetry
Kreamer, PA 17833

About the Author

Author Jane Moss Snow is a respected home builder, interior designer, and author.

From 1972 to 1978, Ms. Snow was president of DWS Enterprises, Inc., a home building company that constructed single-family residences in New York and Virginia. During this period, Ms. Snow, a cooking authority, published *A Family Harvest* (Bobbs Merrill), which was chosen as a *Better Homes & Gardens* Cookbook of the Month in 1976.

Ms. Snow also presided over her own interior design business in New York and Southampton. She studied at the New York School of Interior Design and apprenticed with Clifford Stanton Interiors of New York.

In addition, Ms. Snow was Director of Public Affairs for Home Owners Warranty Corporation (HOW) from 1978 to 1985. She is an authority on construction quality control and HOW's warranty insurance program for new single-family homes.

Ms. Snow has been an interior design feature writer for the Gannett News Service, serving 90 newspapers nationwide. Her articles have also appeared in *National Geographic, Parade Magazine, Mortgage Banker, Mid-Atlantic Country, Medical Economics,* and *Challenge!* Ms. Snow is also the author of *Kitchens*, published by the National Association of Home Builders.

Contents

Chapter 1—Introduction 7
  Baths in the Past 7
  Bathrooms Today 9

Chapter 2—Bathroom Location 13
  The Master Bath 13
  The Second Bath 15
  The Half Bath 15
  The Bath for the Elderly and/or Handicapped 16
  Cost-efficient Plumbing 16

Chapter 3—Fixtures 19
  Bathtubs 20
  Spas 22
  Showers 23
  Steam Baths 24
  Saunas 24
  Lavatories 25
  Toilets 27
  Bidets 29

Chapter 4—Fittings and Accessories 31
  Fittings 31
  Accessories 33

Chapter 5—Countertops, Walls, and Floors 37
  Ceramic Tile 37
  Wood 41
  Marble 41
  Granite 41
  Cultured Marble and Onyx 41
  Solid Plastics 42
  Laminates 42
  Paint and Wallpaper 43
  Mirrors 43
  Carpeting 43
  Resilient Flooring 45
  Ceilings 46

Chapter 6—Lighting, Heating, Ventilation, and Insulation ... 47
  Lighting 47
    Natural Light 47
    Artificial Light 50
    The Uses of Bathroom Lighting 50
  Heating 51
  Ventilation 51
  Insulation and Noise Control 52

Chapter 7—Storage 53
  Use Walls for Storage 57
  Euro-style Versus Traditional Cabinet Construction 57
  Cabinet Materials 58
  Space-expanding Ideas 59

Chapter 8—How to Design a Bathroom 61
    Help With Bathroom Design 61
    Principles of Bath Design 62
    The Floor Plan 67

Chapter 9—The Basic Bathroom 85

Chapter 10—The Move-up Bathroom 91
    Who Are the Move-up Buyers? 91
    Designing a Move-up Bath 92

Chapter 11—Designing for the Elderly and Handicapped 101
    The Market 101
    General Design Requirements 102
        Access 102
        Safety 105

Appendix 1—Plumbing System Materials 107

Appendix 2—Fixture Materials 109

Appendix 3—Detailed Information on Lighting, Ventilation, and Insulation 113
    Lighting the Bathroom 113
    Ventilating the Bathroom 115
    Insulating the Bathroom 115

Appendix 4—Templates and Graph Paper 118

References 124

Chapter 1

Introduction

Baths in the Past

Today the bathroom is such an integral part of the house that it is hard to believe that the number of sanitary fixtures (mostly tubs and lavatories) produced in 1923 was under 5 million in the United States. And this was double the number produced in 1921. Annual production today is approximately 28 million (Bureau of the Census 1986).

As recently as 1958, 42 million (or 84 percent of) U.S. homes had television sets; only 41 million had bathrooms (Television Digest, Inc. 1958). In fact, the Bureau of the Census reported that 2.2 million homes in the United States were still without bathrooms in 1986.

Most people are familiar with the sophistication of the ancient Roman baths that served the vast reaches of the Roman Empire (Figure 1). Although the wealthy enjoyed private baths, everyone used the magnificent public edifices. The Romans enjoyed their baths, considering them social gatherings and an integral part of their lives, if not their community duty. Prior to his murder in AD 217, Emperor Caracalla built baths that accommodated 1,600 at once and covered an area six times as large as St. Paul's Cathedral in London (Figure 2).

Not to be outdone, Diocletian built baths that were reputedly twice as large. Their vestibule was converted by Michelangelo into the huge church of S. Maria degli Angeli in Rome.

Roman water closets and public latrines were flushed by water, a great contribution to clean and fragrant air that was not to be equalled again until Queen Victoria's day.

When the Roman Empire fell, bathing fell with it. The conquerors seem to have been too primitive to absorb the many civilized practices of the Romans, from road and home building to sanitation. In England people actually painted themselves blue, and it is doubtful that they combed their hair.

What efforts at bathing that remained were nurtured by the monasteries, and these must have been appalling by our standards. *Clean and Decent*, Lawrence Wright's excellent history of bathing, describes the English monastery bathing routine as follows: "The Chamberlain had to provide fresh straw for the mattresses once a year. He had to buy wood to keep up the fire in the 'calefactory' or warming-room and to provide warm water and soap for baths two, three, or even four times a year, for head-shaving every three weeks, and for foot-washing on Saturdays" (Wright 1960).

Figure 1. Ancient Roman bath

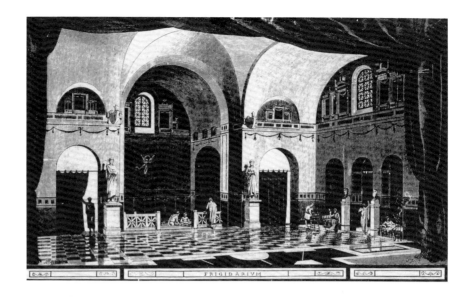

Figure 2. Caracalla's Bath in Rome

It is astounding that none of the victorious Angles and Saxons in England appreciated the luxury of the hot water at Bath or the convenience of the water-flushed latrines in the soldiers' barracks. (Even the art of making bricks and pipe was lost, to be rediscovered in another 1,000 years.)

Millions were still bathing habitually on Saturday nights through the 1930s; so, great advances have been made in bathrooms in just the last 50 years.

From a "necessary," as a toilet was once called, and a tub, which might have been anything from a tin washtub to a copper bathtub, the bathroom changed into a 5-foot × 7-foot, three-fixture room tucked between two bedrooms. This was its 20th century configuration until recently.

The best that can be said of most baths is that they served their purposes. Many who grew up before World War II remember homes where one such bath served eight or ten people.

Bathrooms Today

Today, bathrooms are receiving their just due. Figures show that 47 percent of all new single-family homes had two bathrooms, while 33 percent had two and a half or more (Bureau of the Census 1986).

In one 1985 study, 42.1 percent of consumers surveyed wanted two baths, and 23 percent wanted two and a half. Another 7.7 percent specified three, and 3.9 percent preferred three and a half or more (National Association of Home Builders 1985). What percentage of respondents were satisfied with one bath? Just 4.2 percent—and this figure is skewed by the high percentage of elderly buyers included in the figures.

The number of baths consumers prefer, while important, is only a cold statistic in a sizzling market. What is exciting consumers and selling homes today is the kind of bathrooms those statistics represent.

A clear picture of consumer preferences emerges from a look at the remodeling market, where bathrooms are a major growth area, according to a survey conducted in 1986 (*Kitchen and Bath Design News* 1986).

This survey shows that about 60 percent of bathroom remodeling jobs include whirlpool tubs. On the East Coast, this figure is 71.9 percent. Bidets are requested by 32 percent, saunas/steam baths by 26 percent. Ceramic tile is the choice of 72.9 percent and cultured marble, of 60.9 percent (*Kitchen and Bath Design News* 1986).

The bathroom has become a way for the home owner to make a personal statement—much more than just a room off the master bedroom. (See Figure 3.) The Romans would approve.

Figure 3. This bath, custom-designed for a stockbroker, is equipped with a ticker that can be viewed from the tub.

Courtesy Kohler

Figure 4. This bath has an entertainment area, spa, and greenhouse window.

Courtesy Kohler

Social and economic conditions are responsible for the bathroom's heightened status. Among these is increased numbers of women in the workplace.

Approximately two-thirds of all married women between the ages of 35 and 44 are working, while a majority of married women of all ages work outside the home. It is estimated that 28 percent of the households between the ages of 35 and 44 have annual earnings exceeding $35,000 (The Conference Board 1987); furthermore, this group's spending power will increase almost twice as fast as that of the total population (National Association of Home Builders 1985).

Working women have specific daily needs that must be met. No longer can a woman wait until her male counterpart has left for work to shower or attend to her dressing. Baths must accommodate two adults in the morning. Children's baths should also serve two or more. This means double sinks, tubs and separate showers, dressing rooms, and other amenities.

In addition, the stress of coping with an accelerated pace of life is creating a need for ways to relax and get away from it all—right in your own home. The upscale bathroom or spa is an answer. Complete with whirlpools, total environment units, exercise equipment, and lounging chairs, the bath becomes a refuge and an entertainment center (Figure 4). Spurred by the hot tub craze, companionable relaxation in whirlpools has become a popular pastime.

Another factor affecting bath construction is the aging of the population. The number of people over 65 is growing at the rate of 24 percent (Bureau of the Census 1983). Not only is the population getting older, but there are more very old people: the number of those aged 85 and up will more than double in the last two decades of this century (Bureau of the Census 1983).

This change in our population will also create a demand for changes in bathroom design. As more and more retirement homes and communities are built, better ways to equip them must be developed. Not all

Figure 5. The surge of interest in Victoriana has encouraged manufacturers to produce claw-footed tubs.

Courtesy Kohler

of the need is for the handicapped; it is also for those who are just not as agile as they once were.

The revolution in bathroom design is spawning an exciting new range of products, many of them long overdue from a safety standpoint. Faucets are available that prevent sudden surges of scalding water and that provide a constant, controlled temperature. Swivel faucets can be extended to accommodate hair washing or filling of deep vessels. Easily managed controls for arthritic hands are available that are just as handsome as those for healthy ones, while styles run the gamut from whimsical animal heads to elegant gold plate.

Besides whirlpools, there are soft bathtubs that cushion the body, tubs with armrests, square tubs, claw-footed, Victorian-style tubs—something to please any taste and preference in comfort. (See Figure 5.)

The aesthetics of the bath have become so important that leading manufacturers have banded together to offer color coordinates in everything from basic plumbing fixtures to the tile, towels, and rugs. Eljer Plumbing even provides a complete bathroom design service—from floor plans to wallpaper. These services make builders' and customers' lives much simpler.

New cabinetry has also hit the bathroom market. The Euro-style, frameless designs, increasingly popular in kitchens, are moving into the bathroom as well, adding easier maintenance, as well as more storage area.

Furthermore, technological advances are affecting bath design. For example, a new generation of cultured marble and onyx used for lavatories and counters has properties that allow for an endless array of colors and textures, dramatically changing the look of upscale baths.

One of the most important trends is the melding of the bedroom with the bath. The bedroom may open directly into the larger bath, or it may feed into a dressing area and then into the bath. Separate dressing areas for male and female occupants, complete with sinks and toilet compartments, separate bathing facilities, and a shared spa are features of the upscale home today.

Good bath design is crucial to home sales: survey after survey reveals that impressive bathrooms excite buyers and sell homes. This guide will help in planning and building such bathrooms by providing appealing floor plans, information on where to obtain expert design assistance, spatial requirements, storage, and the latest on fixtures, fittings, and accessories. It also tells you how lighting, both natural and artificial, is used to enhance baths. Chapters devoted to designing for special markets, such as those for the basic home, move-up home, and homes for the elderly and handicapped, are included. In addition, the book contains specific requirements for providing adequate plumbing, heating, and ventilation.

Chapter 2

Bathroom Location

When homes had only one bathroom, location was simple: between two bedrooms, with the door opening into the hall. A second bath was usually a powder room tucked under the stairs in the front hall or behind the kitchen.

Thoughtful design has changed all that, as has the increase in the number of bathrooms. With more than 76 percent of new home buyers preferring two or more baths, user needs dictate location decisions. Suites of rooms are becoming the preferred configuration, where baths and bedrooms are planned as units rather than as two boxes side by side.

Bathrooms in the average two-bath home with children must be cannily designed so that two people in the bathroom can function as efficiently as one. One bath must be placed conveniently to serve more than one bedroom.

"Amenity" bathrooms, such as powder rooms, pool baths, and children's "mudroom" baths must be positioned for the most convenience. A powder room located in the front entrance hall is no longer an acceptable solution in most homes.

Bathrooms should be located away from major traffic flow areas, if possible, to provide greater privacy for family and guests. Today people want to handle their bodily functions in private, sharing only the pleasures of bathing.

The flushing of toilets should not echo down the hall. Nor should the whine of an electric razor or the whir of a hair dryer interfere with conversation in the living room or sleep in the adjacent bedroom. Quiet is possible with careful placement of fixtures against sound-deadening walls, insulation, and acoustical materials.

The Master Bath

In any home with two or more baths, one should be integrated into the master bedroom suite and have its own private entrance. Even in a modest home, the master bath offers the builder an opportunity to enhance the marketability of the home through good design.

The master suite is a key preference item among home buyers (*Professional Builder* 1986). Of those surveyed in one study, 75 percent preferred a private bath; 73 percent, a walk-in closet; and 12.5 percent preferred the bath separated from other bedrooms. Almost 44 percent of those surveyed wanted an oversized bath, and 23 percent responded that they actually needed one that was oversized (*Professional Builder* 1986).

Table 1 lists other bathroom features that respondents to this survey preferred:

Table 1. Preferred Bathroom Features

Preferred Feature	Percentage of Respondents
Medicine cabinet	90.6
Exhaust fans	81.5
Linen cabinets	80.7
Tub/shower door	69.7
Single-bowl vanity	58.3
Ceramic tile floor	53.6
Ceramic tile walls	51.0
Colored fixtures	41.2
Safety features	39.2
Bathroom heater	38.4
Double-bowl vanity	33.4
White fixtures	32.8

Figure 6. His and her bath

Courtesy Wood-Mode Cabinetry

Although the double-bowl vanity was less preferred in this survey than the single-bowl type, the double-bowl vanity has sales appeal among all markets, along with ceramic tile floors and separate showers (*Builder* 1986).

Since the majority of women are working, the master bath in all types of homes should be planned for simultaneous use by a woman and a man (Figure 6). A bath should allow two people room for bathing and dressing, without having to stumble over each other or take turns. Even in more modest homes, such features as separate dressing rooms, compartmentalized fixtures, double sinks, and shower/tub facilities are becoming more common. These additions make a home look more expensive and desirable.

A dressing area should be a major consideration in the master bath. If it is incorporated into the bath itself, include access to the closets and a make-up area. Mirrored closet doors are a natural in such rooms: they provide convenience while creating a sense of space. When facing a mirrored vanity wall, the double mirror yields a spectacular-looking room with enormous practicality. And mirrors are another consumer preference. In addition, storage and cabinet space should be a part of the dressing area or adjacent to it. Vanities should include storage space, not simply an open space below the lavatory.

In a move-up home the master bath should be a well-thought-out retreat for the home owner, with as many modern amenities as possible.

Luxury homes should have his and her baths, although a whirlpool and/or exercise-entertainment center may be shared.

The master bath need not be just a room attached to the bedroom. Thoughtful placement of closets and dressing space, as well as open bathing areas, can turn two rooms into a spacious suite that looks great and functions well.

The Second Bath

The placement of the second bath depends on the market for which you are building. Is the home intended for the young adult market with children? Is your target the empty nester? Each segment of the market has specific preferences and needs.

Homes with children need baths that serve several individuals at once. Careful design and the addition of an extra sink and compartments make a bath multifunctional. Separate the lavatories from the rest of the bath. Put the water closet in a private room, if possible. This goes a long way toward eliminating the morning line-up for the bathroom.

If space permits, turning one more generous bath into two smaller ones is an ideal solution, especially for two teenagers. In this case one bath should open from a bedroom and one from a hallway. Plan adequate storage space for towels, sheets, and other necessities.

Ideally, laundry facilities should be located adjacent to the second bath, where dirty clothes can be conveniently tossed. Since the bulk of the laundry consists of sheets and towels, this location saves time and energy. This arrangement is particularly desirable in two-story homes. If this design isn't possible, then provide a chute from the second bathroom or adjacent to it to the laundry room.

In empty-nester homes or those for young professionals or upwardly mobile executives, the second bath will usually be for transient use or for guests. It must be conveniently located for the guest room, as well as for use from the living areas of the home.

The second bath in this case may open from the hallway or from the second bedroom. If it is supposed to serve two bedrooms, the bath should open from the hallway.

In a home with a half bath (discussed below), the guest bath need not serve the living area and can be positioned more conveniently to the guest area and removed further from the living area.

The guest bath should provide ample storage space for towels, guest linens, and other necessities; it should offer dressing space, if possible, as well as a make-up area. A whirlpool puts the guest bath into the luxury category.

The Half Bath

The half bath or powder room is highly desirable in move-up homes. It relieves the traffic for the second bath and can be more convenient than one placed further away from the living area.

The half bath should not be placed beside the front door, opening into the front hall. This not only obstructs traffic flow, as users and arriving guests collide, but it presents an acoustical problem as well.

In addition, a bathroom must be placed so that those in the living room or dining room do not have a clear visual shot of it when the door is open. Who wants to sit in the living room and stare at a toilet?

The half bath is a convenience for guests, and it should be designed and decorated with that in mind. Too often it's so small that imaginative decorating is all that can be done. Even the smallest room can provide good light, ample shelving for make-up repairs, and storage for towels, paper, and soap (Figure 7). Too many half baths consist of a toilet, sink, mirror, and light, with no place to put a handbag, rest a comb, or dispose of a used tissue.

The powder room should be convenient to a coat closet, (preferably

Figure 7. A powder room with plenty of storage

Courtesy Wilsonart

one with ample space for boots, umbrellas, and hats) for last-minute needs before leaving the house.

In homes that have pools but no lanai or poolhouse, a half bath (or full one) should be conveniently located to an outside door to prevent people from walking in and out of the house while dripping wet. Or provide access directly from the bath to the outside, as is commonly done in Florida. This is the ideal place to provide for guest dressing as well. A bath with easy access to the outside is especially convenient for families with children. Storage for boots, coats, and outdoor toys should be adjacent.

If a half bath must be used as the guest powder room, as well as for people coming in and out, provide a general cloak/dressing room beside it to help maintain neatness.

When the laundry is not placed beside the second bath, placing it beside a half bath is a good second choice. In one-story homes, this may be the best solution.

The Bath for the Elderly and/or Handicapped

If a home is designed for use by the elderly and/or handicapped, the bath should be conveniently located near the bedroom, with easy access to the kitchen and living areas. This requires careful attention to dimensions of halls, doorways, and the interior of the room itself. (See Chapter 11.)

Without sufficient space, a bathroom cannot be adapted for a wheelchair at a later date. Widening doorways or halls can be prohibitively expensive, but adding the extra inches in the beginning is simple and costs little or nothing.

Cost-efficient Plumbing

Designing the home so that the baths, kitchen, and laundry plumbing ties into one wet wall is the most cost-effective approach. This is most easily achieved in a two-story structure or a tightly contained one-story design. By shifting a fixture's location, it may be possible to install one stack instead of two in some cases. These economies are the benefits of careful planning.

Larger homes, particularly sprawling ones, require more than one plumbing stack. The variety of plumbing fixtures has increased tremendously, requiring more planning of the plumbing system. Items such as whirlpools, steam baths, and saunas need special plumbing and electrical systems. Check manufacturers' specifications prior to construction.

An illustration of a residential plumbing system appears in Figure 8. Water enters the house through the supply pipes, also called pressure pipes because they must be able to handle a specific level of pressure expressed in p.s.i., pounds per square inch. Since water must be supplied to all levels of the house, pressure is exerted through a pump or other means.

Supply pipes separate into hot and cold water pipes when diverging from the main supply line, with the hot water piping feeding through the water heater.

The drain system is controlled by gravity rather than by pressure; hence, the phrase "down the drain." Some more sophisticated systems, however, have pumps. DWV, which stands for drain, waste, and vent, is used to designate the drain system. This term differentiates such piping from other types.

An essential element in plumbing is the vent pipe. Designed to prevent gases and odors from escaping into the home by providing for it through the roof, vent pipe allows draining water to get air without siphoning off the trap.

By maintaining equal pressure on the system, water remains in the plumbing traps of each fixture, forming a seal that prevents gases from entering the room. (The toilet is the only fixture with a built-in trap.) Without venting, water would be siphoned off, and the gases would penetrate the bath and home. Local codes are extremely strict about the distances between vents and traps.

Prefabricated plumbing systems are available and were once the target of high expectations but proved impractical for single-family homes due to the many variations in floor plans. They are useful in multifamily construction.

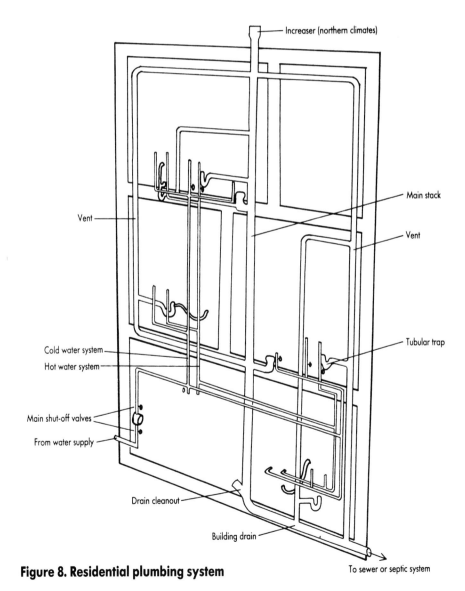

Figure 8. Residential plumbing system

Courtesy College of Product Knowledge

Figure 9. Forerunners of the modern-day toilet

Chapter 3

Fixtures

Almost 4,000 years ago on the island of Crete, the queen bathed in a tub shaped remarkably like those of modern times; two light wells diffused and reflected the light and kept the air fresh in her toilet. Other Cretan baths at a public inn had running water, plugs, and waste pipes.

In all cases through the centuries, the bath was in a bathing room, while the water closet and lavatory were elsewhere. Examples of these ancient bathing rooms can be seen at Hampton Court and Leeds Castle in England. Tubs might be made of copper, marble, or tin. Bathing rooms for royalty were elaborate, magnificently decorated rooms, although they were poorly plumbed.

The common folk, however, seldom if ever bathed even into this century, and the bathtub and wash basin were portable. The tub was generally lugged into the kitchen, where the family used it in front of the hearth, often without changing the water between baths.

Stone basins, known as lavers, lavabos, or lavatoria, were used for personal washing. These might be in a public or private chamber and often were supplied from a cistern mounted above them. Eventually, wooden lavabos or washstands became showcases of the cabinetmaker's art.

Whether called a water closet, as in the plumbing trade, or a toilet, as many manufacturers term it, this fixture has a long, unsavory history. Having disappeared, along with the rest of Roman plumbing, toilets were not to reemerge until the 19th century.

Pots concealed in elaborate chairs served the wealthy, whose servants emptied them. Slops were tossed out the windows to the peril of anyone walking by.

When indoor toilets were installed, they were simply holes opening into shafts leading to sewers, without any flushing facility. (See Figure 9.) Joseph Bramah, an English cabinetmaker, perfected a valve that worked on a flush toilet in 1778. This was the standard toilet used for the next 100 years; it was not vented for gases and sometimes even exploded.

Bathroom fixtures have evolved a long way from the chamberpot and the washstand. New materials, manufacturing know-how, and better understanding of the human body have combined to produce fixtures that are more convenient, easier to use and to clean, and more versatile.

Whirlpools are psychologically and physically relaxing. An antidote to the pressures of daily living, they are the centerpieces of relaxation rooms, where entertaining may be done. This change in approach to baths makes small, enclosed bathrooms a thing of the past.

Among the technological advancements in bathrooms are electronic controls. They appear in the bath as remote controls for filling whirlpools and as temperature controls for faucets. These eliminate the need to adjust the faucets with each use. Even more important, they prevent sudden scaldings from cascading water.

Another breakthrough in this country is the understanding and acceptance of the bidet as a sanitary perineal cleansing aid, rather than as a symbol of illicit sex. More than 32 percent of remodeling jobs reported in one nationwide dealer/designer survey in 1986 involved installing bidets (*Kitchen and Bath Design News* 1986).

Advances have been made in the design and the materials used in most parts of the bathroom. Fixtures are shaped to fit the body, providing greater comfort and easier use. Special designs accommodate children and the handicapped. Technological advances are providing strong, light materials that can be molded and contoured, making installation simple and eliminating such problems as leaks and mold and mildew.

The following paragraphs describe bathroom fixtures—tubs, spas, showers, steam baths, saunas, lavatories, toilets, and bidets—their various styles, sizes, and features.

Bathtubs

The tub is the first fixture installed in the bath and must be put in place after the rough-in stage. After installation, tubs should be carefully covered to prevent damage during construction. A chipped tub can mean a costly repair or replacement. Workmen should not be permitted to stand in a tub without using a sturdy cover to prevent scratching and gouging.

There is something for everyone in the way of tubs. Builders of nostalgic Victorian-like homes are installing new claw-footed tubs. These may also work well in the guest bath, while the master suite is equipped with a whirlpool with all the latest gadgets. Tubs are available that are large enough for two or more, curved to fit the body, with seats, remote controls, and in practically any shape you can think of.

Tubs are available with grab bars built in and with slip-resistant bottoms. Drains may be located at either end.

Sizes generally range from 14 to over 20 inches deep, 23½ to 44 inches wide, and 4 to 6 or more feet long. Special sizes and shapes are available. Whirlpool models come in standard as well as special sizes.

It is important to check the interior dimensions of the tub. For two people to sit side by side, a minimum width of 42 inches is needed inside the tub, and it must be at least 20 inches deep. Inner dimensions must be checked because overlarge ledges may reduce seating space. Steps up to a platformed tub should have at least a 10-inch step and a 7-inch riser.

The following describes the six types of basic tub styles: recessed, free-standing, square, sunken, whirlpool, and receptor.

The recessed tub is finished on one side and fits into the walls on the remaining three sides. It is available in porcelain enameled cast iron, steel, plastics, and exotic materials.

Porcelain enameled cast iron is the most popular material for this type of tub. A recessed tub of this material (as does a porcelain enameled steel tub) usually requires a ledger piece or special hangers to prevent its pulling away from the wall. Acrylic/fiberglass tubs may have nailing straps that are affixed to the studs.

Recessed tubs with the water supply lines concealed in the wall are used for showers. One-piece plastic units combining tub and shower are also available and make construction simpler.

Free-standing tubs are finished on all four sides and may be placed anywhere in the room. Generally, they have higher sides and may be larger than other tubs. The copies of Victorian claw-footed tubs are an example of free-standing units. Contemporary styles are also available.

Square tubs may be tucked into a corner or be recessed in an alcove. Completely skirted styles can be placed in the middle of a room.

Sunken tubs may be completely enclosed with decorative material on four sides or flushed against one or two walls (Figure 10). They may be surrounded with tile, marble, cast acrylic, or various other materials and placed on a platform to be approached by steps or slightly recessed below the floor, with only one step.

Figure 10. A sunken tub with tiled surrounds is elevated for emphasis. Note the mirrored wall and plant shelf.

Courtesy West and Associates, Architects

Figure 11. This luxury bath features a whirlpool that is recessed flush with the floor.

Courtesy Jacuzzi, Inc.

A sunken tub becomes an integral part of the bath, rather than an addition to it, creating a sense of space and airiness. Once considered only for the luxury market, they may be used to add sales appeal to more moderately priced homes also.

Sunken tubs have lipped edges that fit over the surrounds. Many have optional front panels. They are available in a variety of shapes: round, oval, rectangular, square, octagonal, and even heart and kidney shaped.

Sunken tubs also come in a mind-boggling array of sizes. Generally, they range from 40 to 83 inches wide, 48 to 108 inches long, and 16 to 39 inches deep. They accommodate from one to eight people, and those large enough for two are readily available in most lines. Most sunken tubs are available with whirlpools.

Developed by Roy Jacuzzi 30 years ago, whirlpools were once toys for the rich. Less expensive versions of the whirlpool were introduced in the early 1980s and found their way into the development home. Their pumping systems have been improved; water jets can be directed at will; electronic controls operate with a touch; the hissing and whining have been eliminated, and fashion colors are available. Other leading manufacturers are now offering these tubs, along with Jacuzzi® Whirlpool Bath. Now whirlpools are available in recessed or sunken tubs, and there is something in a whirlpool for everyone (Figure 11).

Since each manufacturer's line is different, the pump may be located on either end of the tub. Planning for a whirlpool requires including room for the pump and easy access to it.

Note that controls must be located away from the tub to prevent electrical accidents. Fixtures with microprocessor controls or air control switches in the tub prevent contact with any electrical controls.

Most whirlpool baths are made of plastic with slip-resistant finishes for safety. Pumps, air-intake systems, jets, and suction fittings are integrated into the tub. Weight varies depending on size; check with the manufacturer or distributor prior to construction. Larger whirlpools require different plumbing. The ½-inch pipe used for standard tubs and fixtures is insufficient for larger tubs and whirlpools. Use ¾-inch supply line pipe with a ¾-inch IPS (iron pipe size) valve and bath spout.

Receptor tubs, used primarily for bathing children or invalids, are usually about 4 square feet and 12 inches deep. They are also used as shower bases and are made of porcelain enameled cast iron or steel or plastic with slip-resistant surfaces.

Spas

The spa differs from the whirlpool in that its water, which is filtered and cleaned as in a swimming pool, remains in it. A whirlpool, however, is emptied after each use as is any tub.

The spa began as an outdoor hot tub made of redwood or cedar in a barrel shape. Today spas are found both indoors and out, and portable units are being manufactured. They are made of materials ranging from tile to stone to plastic.

Spas are deeper than tubs and use heated water that is thermostatically controlled. Whirlpools are typical accessories. Spas vary in size to accommodate 1 or 2 or up to 8 to 10 people. They use gas or electric heaters with 110-volt or 220-volt connections requiring 20 to 90 amps. All electrical hook-ups must have ground fault circuit interrupter (GFCI) breakers at the service main or built into the fixture. Skimmers and filters are essential equipment.

Showers

Whirlpools and spas do not eliminate the need for a shower, since cleansing showers are usually taken before using either of these.

Separate showers are a must in today's culture. Often thought of as male-oriented, they are preferred by many women as the ideal cleansing fixture.

As noted, showers are generally incorporated into the recessed tub area, with the plumbing concealed in the wall. The supply lines and drain serve both fixtures.

Stall showers may be custom tiled or molded fiberglass units, which are installed over receptors that are approximately 4½ inches deep.

Custom receptors (usually tile) are laid on a lead pan or vinyl liner and must have a ¼-inch-per-foot slope to ensure proper drainage of water. Prefabricated units have a built-in slope. All methods of construction require a watertight bond between the receptor and the wall unit.

All receptors should have non-slip surfaces. Prefabricated fiberglass units are available with grab bars, accessory shelves, and seats.

Showers on exterior walls require vapor barriers and special insulation to prevent frozen pipes.

Typical prefabricated unit sizes in inches are as follows: 32 inches wide × 36 inches deep × 73 inches high, 36 inches wide × 36 inches deep × 73 inches high, and 48 inches wide × 36 inches deep × 73 inches high. Heights vary depending on the manufacturer. A model for the handicapped with a ramp 64 inches wide × 64 inches deep × 73 inches high is available.

Place the shower faucet controls near the entry. This prevents sudden surges of hot water when adjusting the faucets. They should be operable from inside and outside the shower.

Shower seats should be the width of the enclosure and should be placed on the dry end of the shower opposite the controls. All seats should be 15 inches from the floor. A footrest in the shower should also be 15 inches from the floor and measure a minimum of 6 inches × 6 inches.

The preferred shower size is 72 inches high, 42 wide, and 36 inches deep. A 30-inch width does not allow sufficient room for bending over. It should be noted that the National Standard Plumbing Code specifies a minimum width of 30 inches for a shower entryway. Local codes may differ.

Doors must not interfere with access to the faucets from the exterior, nor should they block access to the dry end of the shower (Kira 1967).

Prefabricated showers generally have ledge space built in. In custom-built showers, make sure to provide the following:

- Soap holder/grab bar
- Shampoo shelf (12 to 15 inches long × 4 inches deep) placed 40 inches from the floor
- Brush hook
- Washcloth hook
- Towel hook by the entry

Steam Baths

Steam baths can be incorporated in the shower or tub area (Figure 12) or added as separate fixtures. If a steam bath is going to be included, the room or area must be vapor proof.

The steam bath requires a ¼-inch copper tube steam line to handle the 120-degree-heat of the water. In addition, a heater must be installed. Steam supply lines should be installed with a downward pitch to drain the condensation. They should enter the tub area 6 inches above the ledge of the tub. In the shower, they should enter 12 inches above the floor and opposite the spot where the user stands.

Steam baths require vapor-proof sliding doors, when installed in tubs, or a hinged shower door. It must be enclosed to the ceiling. Seating must also be included.

Steam baths require a separate 220-volt circuit. The timer must be at least 5 feet away from the enclosure. A device to limit the amount of time for the steam bath must be inside the enclosure.

Saunas

The sauna has been a favorite of the Scandinavians, who leap from the heat into a snow bank. Depending on dry heat and low humidity of approximately 15 percent, the sauna is an insulated room usually made of kiln-dried western cedar (Figure 13), which resists staining, is easy to clean with soap and water, retains its stability, and has a low surface temperature.

Rooms should provide a minimum of 4 square feet per person; 6 feet is preferable. Heaters require 240 volts for large rooms and 120 volts

for smaller ones. No electrical connections can be placed inside the room, according to UL requirements.

Saunas must have non-locking doors that swing out, a protective fence around the heater, tempered safety glass for windows, and UL-approved temperature controls, timers, and safety cut-offs. In addition, rooms must have R11 insulation, and benches should be of western cedar.

The new tempered glass doors are very popular because they relieve the claustrophobia that some people feel when in an enclosed sauna.

Figure 13. A sauna is incorporated into the master bedroom; the glass door and wall make the space open and inviting.

Courtesy Amerec

Lavatories

The lavatory or wash basin is the second of the three essential fixtures in the minimum bathroom. The lavatory and the toilet are the two essential powder room fixtures.

The three types of lavatories are the wall-hung model, the integral lavatory, and the drop-in lavatory (Figure 14).

Wall-hung models are those units that are attached to the wall with a metal bracket with strong supports concealed inside the wall to carry the weight. Better designs conceal the plumbing in the basic bowl design. Styles of wall-hung sinks are the slab, ledge, backsplash, and pedestal.

Sizes range from 13 inches wide × 13 inches deep to 24 inches wide × 21 inches deep.

Wall-hung models come with backsplashes or flush tops. The flat area for placing items is limited, so choose models with at least 4 inches of ledge area.

Pedestal sinks are enjoying a resurgence in popularity and are

Figure 14. Types of lavatories

Courtesy College of Product Knowledge

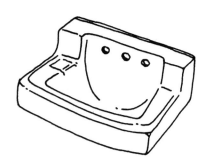

LEDGE

CABINET TOP

SLAB

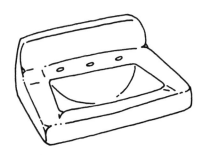

BACK-SPLASH

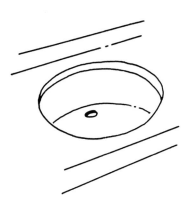

UNDER COUNTER

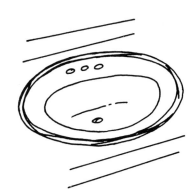

EXTERNAL FRAME

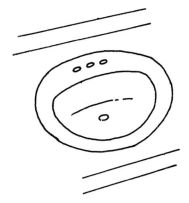

SELF-RIMMING

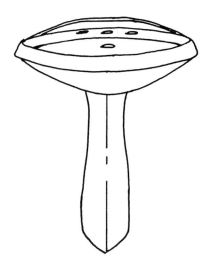

PEDESTAL

available in handsome new styles. Since they lack large ledges or integrated storage areas, make sure to provide necessary shelves and storage with this sink. These sinks hide the plumbing, and bowl sizes are as large as 47⅝ inches wide × 23¼ inches deep.

The usual bowl height is 31 inches from the floor, but many people find this too low. The preferred height is 34 to 36 inches (Kira 1967). In custom-built homes the height should be in accordance with the buyers' preferences. Pedestal models have fixed heights, usually of 32 inches.

Integral lavatories are molded in one piece with the countertop and are placed on a vanity base. They range from a narrow, 16-inch top to double-bowl models. They are also available with extended counters. In materials such as Corian®, Avonite®, and Formica 2000X®, they can be shaped using woodworking tools.

The majority of molded lavatories are of cultured marble. Cultured onyx, vitreous china, and other new materials are also available in a variety of shapes, including shells, and in many colors.

The integral lavatory has the advantage of a single surface that makes cleaning easier. No-drip edges are available. Avoid flat tops, on which the water puddles rather than runs off.

The drop-in lavatory is fit into a countertop that has a cut out. It may be dropped in from above or mounted below. Types of drop-in sinks are the external frame, undercounter, and self-rimming styles.

The self-rimming lavatory in vitreous china is the most popular. It drops into the cut out and rims the vanity top. It is secured with retaining clips that fasten it to the countertop and is caulked around the rim to prevent seepage.

Self-rimming models range from 21 inches × 13 inches to 38 inches × 22 inches. Most take faucets with water supply holes 4 or 8 inches on center. They are also available with offset faucet mountings and with countertop mountings. Caulking should match the bowl or countertop.

Rimmed lavatories are the least expensive and are usually made of porcelain enamel on steel. They drop in and are then rimmed with a steel band secured by steel clips. They come in sizes ranging from 17 inches × 14 inches to 26 inches × 18 inches. Faucet mounting holes are 4 or 8 inches on center, although countertop mountings are available. Rimmed models are more difficult to clean because debris collects under the rim.

The third style is the under-counter lavatory, which is usually of vitreous china. Mounted from below, the countertop overlaps the bowl proper. Sizes vary from 17 inches × 14 inches to 21¼ inches × 17¼ inches, and faucets must be mounted on the countertop. This style is more difficult to clean than the other styles.

Toilets

The third essential fixture in the bathroom is the water closet, which has been vastly improved over the past decades. According to Dr. Alexander Kira's, *The Bathroom,* which includes a definitive study of human physiology, the natural position to use on the toilet is a squat. The very low toilets now on the market are, therefore, an improvement over the sitting-height designs.

Manufacturers have also improved the flushing systems of toilets. Great improvements have been made in noise control as well. Overall design now makes maintenance easier. Vitreous china continues to be the first choice of material for water closets.

Figure 15. Types of toilet flush action

WASHDOWN

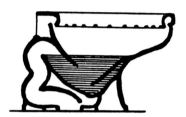

REVERSE TRAP

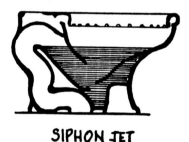

SIPHON JET

Courtesy College of Product Knowledge

The *College of Product Knowledge* recommends that you consider three factors in judging the design of a water closet:

- water surface in the bowl
- depth of water seal (from top of trap to water surface)
- trapway size

In each case in the above, more is better; that is, more water surface, more depth in water seal, and larger passageway (Arnold 1979).

There are four basic types of toilets based on the type of water action: the washdown, the reverse trap, the siphon jet, and the siphon vortex (Figure 15). These are discussed in the following paragraphs.

The washdown toilet is the oldest type and is no longer made in the United States because of its noise and tendency to get soiled and stained. It flushes by a wash-out action and tends to clog.

The reverse trap toilet has replaced the washdown model in inexpensive toilets. This works on a siphonic action created in the trapway and aided by a water jet at the inlet. Water coverage is minimal, and this is the noisiest of the siphon-action toilets.

The siphon jet toilet, the largest-selling type, is quieter and has a larger water surface than the reverse trap. The jet delivers such flow that the siphoning action begins immediately, without any rise in the level of water in the bowl. It is less likely to clog than the washdown or the reverse trap.

The siphon vortex toilet is the most expensive toilet. It is lower than other models, molded in one piece, quieter, and more efficient due to the larger water surface. These are not supposed to clog or overflow because of the powerful siphon action.

The conservation of water is just as important as the conservation of energy. Toilets that require only one and a half gallons per flush and meet standards established by the American National Standards Institute (ANSI) are available. These toilets require smaller pipe, as well.

Smaller pipe is effective in conserving energy with hot water systems. Hot water remains in the pipe after the faucet is shut off. The smaller pipe delivers the hot water to the faucet faster and retains less. This saves the average household 2,000 to 3,000 gallons worth of heated water per year (NAHB National Research Center, telephone interview, April 1987).

Toilets are available in three styles. The one-piece style is molded with tank and bowl together, which makes it easier to clean. Generally available only in siphon jet or siphon vortex styles, these are low-profile units. They are available with insulated sweat-inhibiting flush tanks, water-saving designs that restrict flow to less than the usual 3½ gallons, and in models that operate with low water pressure (30 psi at the inlet valve). These are made in standard or elongated models.

Elongated water closets require a low water supply line. These models are 2 inches longer from front to back than the standard ones, something to consider in a small bathroom.

Close-coupled constructed toilets are those that have separate tanks connected by a pipe. The tank is set directly on the back of the bowl. These come in wall-hung or floor models. The wall-hung model is easier to clean but requires a special drain fitting and carrier or wall-mounted bracket.

A variation of this toilet is the saddle tank, which looks like one-piece construction but is actually close-coupled. The tank straddles the back of the bowl.

Water closet sizes vary from 20 to 24 inches wide × 26 to 33 inches high, with rim heights 15 to 18 inches. Water closets for the elderly or handicapped should be 18 inches high. Depths from front to back range from 26 to 30 inches.

Insulated flush tanks and elongated bowls are available, as are corner models for special applications.

Two-piece models are being made for Victorian-style baths. They have wall-hung tanks with pull-chains for flushing. These require a ⅜-inch supply line and 10- or 12-inch rough-in for the drain.

Bidets

The bidet is becoming more widely accepted in the United States. As Americans have traveled more, both men and women have learned to appreciate the convenience and benefits of its cleansing capabilities.

Bidets are being made to match other fixtures and resemble water closets without the tank or lid (Figures 16 and 17). Some manufacturers are providing lids for them now, perhaps in deference to American attitudes or feelings of delicacy.

The three types of bidets are described in the following paragraphs.

One type has a vertical spray, a fixed water supply from the center of the bowl. The bowl can be filled and must have a vacuum breaker to prevent back siphonage.

The rim-supplied style bidet is filled with water much like a lavatory bowl. This is the least desirable type because of the possibility of cross infection between the genital and anal regions.

The horizontal spray model has its nozzle mounted on the deck of the fixture and delivers a spray to the body. It does not require a vacuum breaker.

Bidets are vitreous china and require a drain with a 1¼-inch trap, a ⅜-inch supply line, and a rough-in varying from 11 to 16 inches, depending on the model. Bidets require the connection of hot and cold supplies similar to those for a lavatory, and most require a vacuum breaker component.

Figure 16. Bidet components

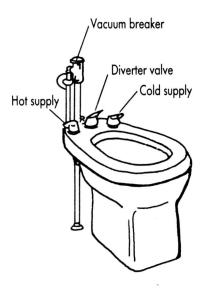

Courtesy College of Product Knowledge

Figure 17. A pedestal lavatory with matching bidet and low profile toilet create a contemporary bath.

Courtesy Villeroy and Boch

Courtesy Artistic Brass

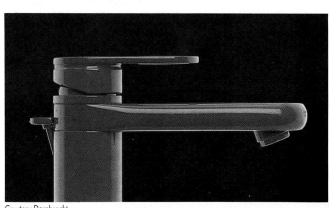

Courtesy Dornbracht

Courtesy Kohler

Courtesy Artistic Brass

Courtesy Kohler

Chapter 4

Fittings and Accessories

The fittings in the bathroom consist of faucets, handles, and valves that control the water supply to the fixtures. A tremendous variety is available today, limited only by cost.

Bathroom accessories include the medicine chest, towel bars, holders of various kinds, shower stall enclosures, and grab bars. There are scales that can be built in, combination toilet paper/brush holders, even electronic controls that will turn on the bath water while the home owner is fighting the freeway traffic.

Selecting handsome, practical fittings and accessories is crucial in creating a bathroom with sales appeal. A multitude of styles, colors, and materials fit any decor—from the most modern to a Victorian reproduction. Hand-painted ceramics, anodized aluminum, gold plate, solid brass, pewter, crystal, and plastic have been added to the standard chrome lines (Figure 18).

Manufacturers are now coordinating broad lines of fittings and accessories with fixtures to make matching the various pieces easier. The blending of styles of heat lamps and other components, however, is still a problem. Be sure it is possible to get items in finishes that are compatible with fittings or that can be painted.

Faucets styled in new, practical ways fulfill a variety of needs and add sales appeal. The moderately priced home can offer some of the more advanced features at little extra cost. The following describes the fittings and accessories available.

Fittings

All fittings on bathroom fixtures should match. As a rule, center-set model faucets for lavatories are installed on the top of the fixture with mounting holes 4 inches apart. Flush mounts are also available.

Widespread faucets, also known as "spread" or "spread centers" usually have 8- or 12-inch centers, although they are available in sizes up to 16 inches. The handles in this type are separated and mounted flush on the surface without a mounting plate. (See Table 2 for faucet and other accessory height requirements.)

Faucets provide the volume and temperature control of the water and come in two basic types: the single-control or single-lever control, introduced around 25 years ago, and the two-handle design (Figure 19).

The single-lever faucet with a side-to-side movement for temperature

Figure 18. Manufacturers are producing faucets in all types of styles, materials, and colors.

Figure 19. Single- and double-lever faucets

Courtesy College of Product Knowledge

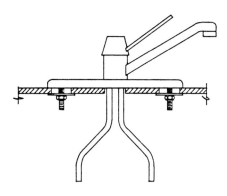

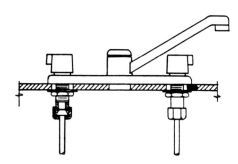

control and back and forth movement for flow rate control is the easiest to operate. Push or pull knobs and screw-action faucets are the most difficult to use.

The two-handle design works by rotation. The single-control, however, works several ways. Some are simple to use, others require more manipulation, so keep this in mind when choosing. Both types of faucets are commonly equipped with a pop-up drain assembly.

The shape of the faucet handle is important for ease in operation. When building for the empty-nester or older market, provide a handle that can be operated with the palm or side of the hand, rather than one that requires finger pressure, which may be painful for arthritic hands.

Faucets that project water out into the bowl are the most efficient because they put the water in the most convenient place for use, especially for hand washing. The high gooseneck conformation is also practical because it is easy to get both hands and head under it.

The swivel, well accepted in the kitchen, is also practical for the bathroom. Shampoo hoses and soap dispensers are now available, as are water flow limiters. Adjustable-height faucets for lavatories have been introduced.

One of the greatest inconveniences and dangers in the bath stems from sudden changes in water temperature due to pressure changes. This is particularly a problem for young children and the elderly or handicapped, who cannot react quickly. Now faucets have been perfected that automatically adjust the water temperature to compensate for changes in pressure. These are available for lavatories, tubs, showers, and bidets.

The newest advance in faucets, appropriate for luxury baths, is the single-handle electronic mixing faucet with a built-in sensor and solar-powered digital readout that measures the water temperature and keeps a constant, even water temperature (Figure 20). These are available for all fixtures.

Better faucets are made with washerless cartridges that do not leak, resist corrosion, and provide years of service. They are also simple to repair because the mechanism or a major part of it is incorporated in the cartridge and can be replaced simply. Washer designs or "compression seal" faucets require a washer and are more prone to leaks.

Figure 20. Faucets are available that automatically measure water temperature.

Courtesy American Standard

Figure 21. Height requirements for faucets and other accessories

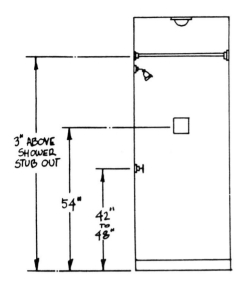

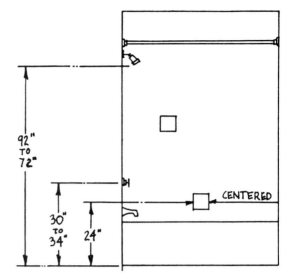

Lavatory and tub faucets can be mounted on the fixture itself or deck mounted. Combined shower and tub faucets are mounted on the wall area around the fixture and should be placed away from the wall containing the showerhead. (See Figure 21 for mounting heights of faucets and other accessories.) This prevents scalding when adjusting the temperature while under flowing water. Although it requires additional piping, the extra safety and convenience are worth the expense.

An NAHB study revealed that 38 percent of consumers surveyed preferred a massage shower head (National Association of Home Builders 1985). The most desirable shower heads provide adjustable sprays that include a wide-angle stream. Water saver devices are a plus. On automatic water temperature control models, one handle controls the flow and the temperature.

Hand-held showers are highly desirable and should always have a wall mount in addition to a mount adjacent to the control faucets, if possible. This permits the user to convert it to a fixed position. In a tub without a shower, the hand-held fitting should be considered. It can also supplement a regular shower, adding the feature of localized cleansing.

Accessories

Accessories styles are keeping pace with those of fittings and fixtures. New shapes, materials, and colors offer the builder wide opportunities to create more attractive, marketable bathrooms that appeal to a wide group of home buyers. Handsome built-ins with a variety of uses are replacing the standard medicine chest, two towel bars, and toilet paper holder. These include tub and shower enclosures, fans, heaters, ventilators, hampers, scales, and intercoms.

The *National Kitchen and Bath Association Bath Design Manual* shows four types of tub and shower enclosures: sliding, folding, hinged, and pivot styles. All-glass enclosures must be made of tempered glass and meet ANSI and the Architectural Glazing Standard safety tests. Designs exist for L-shaped and diagonal corner models. The enclosure must be sized to fit the receptor. Fully round glass enclosures create a handsome free-standing tub and shower unit that is eye catching.

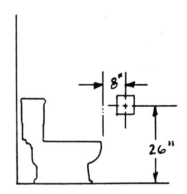

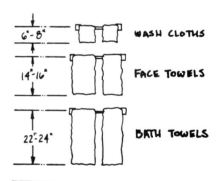

Courtesy National Kitchen and Bath Association

Figure 22. A three-panel medicine cabinet with theatrical-style lights provides extra storage space.

Courtesy Broan

Old-fashioned medicine chests protruded from the wall above the lavatory. Today, the better installations recess them so that they are flat against the wall; or the wall around them is flushed out. Many chests are made with lighting fixtures incorporated. They come with sliding-glass doors, hinged doors, three-way mirrors, and in various types ranging from sleek contemporary units to period styles (Figure 22). The minimum 14-inch size is generally inadequate for storage and for mirror size.

Double chests can be recessed on facing side walls of a vanity area, with the entire center section mirrored. Shallow cabinets can be used to frame a large mirror over a double-bowl vanity. Chests can be used in many ways to increase the storage and convenience in the bathroom. Some designers use vanity space in place of medicine chests. This arrangement, however, is impractical for those who need storage at eye level. Baths for men should never omit eye-level storage. The medicine chest or its equivalent is a sound component of the well-planned bath.

Manufacturers are now fashioning towel bars, toilet paper holders, robe hooks (placed above eye level for safety), glass and toothbrush holders, and soap dishes to coordinate in color and style with fixtures. Attractive styles to complement traditional or modern rooms are available. Ceramic models can be blended with the tile and the fixtures.

Safety, as well as convenience, dictates that every bath have grab bars in the shower, on the tub wall, and adjoining the toilet. Many of the molded shower units and whirlpools have integrated bars. Tiled units, however, must have grab bars added. Unfortunately, most manufacturers do not include bars as part of their accessory lines, so standard bars that detract from a room's beauty are often used. Grab bars should support 250 pounds, be at least 15 inches long, and have a textured gripping surface. They require a firm backing such as 2-inch × 4-inch blocking nailed between the studs or ¾-inch exterior plywood anchored to the stud. Grab bars should be ¾ inch to 1½ inches in diameter and extend at least 1½ inches from the wall. Install grab bars 36 inches above the floor in a shower or 20 inches above the bottom of a 16-inch-deep tub along the back wall. A horizontal bar at least 9 inches long should be in the center of the wall with the tub faucets; or a 9-inch vertical bar should be installed at the entryway into the tub or shower on the wall. Grab bars should be placed adjacent to the toilet and the bidet 33 to 36 inches above the floor. Some manufacturers are offering grab bars for end walls to use with bidets as part of their standard lines.

Table 2 contains the height requirements for mounting fittings and accessories:

Table 2. Fittings and Accessories Height Requirements

Tub/shower faucet combination (one set of faucets only)	30-34″ high
Shower heads	72-78″ high
Shower faucets	42-48″ high
Tub soap dishes	24″ high
Shower soap dishes	54″ high
Toilet paper dispenser	26″ from floor, 8″ from front of toilet
Towel bar space (minimum)	24″ per person
Towel bar/ring	within 6″ of tub/ shower entry/exit
Towel bar hanging space (minimum required)	washcloths—6-8″ face towels—14-16″ bath towels—22-24″
Grab bars (¾ to 1½″ diameter) in tub in shower	1½″ from the wall 16 to 24″ above floor 36 to 48″ above floor

Chapter 5

Countertops, Walls, and Floors

The decorative possibilities for bathroom countertops, walls, and floors are tremendous. Designers are using their ingenuity in baths as much as they are in living rooms, and the results are breathtaking. But they can also be impractical. The key to a successful bathroom is knowing the difference between what's practical and what's not. A case in point is the frequent use of carpeting to skirt tubs and surrounds. It looks great, but water damages such carpeting, and cleaning it is difficult. This chapter deals with materials for countertops, walls, and floors—those surfaces that can transform an ordinary bath into an extraordinary one.

In the days of the Roman Empire, baths were made of marble, stone, and mosaic tile, which proved durable down through the ages. Wood has been used for bathroom walls, floors, and cabinetry, ever since indoor plumbing came about and a special room was set aside for bathing.

In addition to these traditional materials, today's man-made ones offer special advantages to bathroom design. The following describes these materials and their advantages and limitations.

Ceramic Tile

The beauty and durability of tile is apparent in museums, as well as ancient ruins and historic buildings. One of the earliest materials made by man, tile has been used for thousands of years, and the basic method of manufacture is little changed.

Many home buyers prefer tile in baths (Figure 23). In a 1986 consumer/builder survey, 38.3 percent of respondents wanted ceramic tile walls in their bathrooms and were willing to pay more for it (*Professional Builder* 1986).

Unglazed tile owes its color to the clay used and the heat of the firing. It comes in natural colors ranging from tan to deep brick red. It is porous and must be well sealed. Because of the difficulty in sealing and maintenance, unglazed tile is not generally used in bathrooms and should be reserved for customers who specially request it.

Glazed tile has a glazed surface pressed onto it when fired. This gives it a water-resistant surface that is easy to clean, stain proof, and durable. Glazed tile does, however, get scratched over a period of time.

The surface of glazed tile may be glossy, semi-matt, or matt. Floor

Figure 23. A completely tiled tub surrounds and walls add a sense of space to this bath, lit by a skylight.

Courtesy Wenczel

37

tiles should have a slightly abrasive, slip-resistant surface because the glossy finish can be dangerously slick.

Glazed tile is available in squares from 3 inches × 3 inches to 12 inches × 12 inches. It also comes in hexagonal and brick shape and a variety of decorative configurations.

Mosaic tile is the same color all the way through. It is harder and more durable than glazed tile and is stain proof, scratch proof, and is not damaged by cold. It is also less liable to break when something heavy is dropped on it. Generally, ceramic tile is sold in mesh sheets of 12 inches × 12 inches or 12 inches × 24 inches, which makes installation simpler. The tiles themselves are small, usually 1 inch × 1 inch, 2 inches × 2 inches, or 1 inch × 2 inches.

Tile alone will not waterproof shower floors. It must be installed with a special membrane backing material. After the tile is laid, the edges must be finished. Specially trimmed tile is available for corners, transitions between walls and floors, and counter edges.

Tile comes in a variety of styles and patterns. The Tile Council of America, Inc. has guidelines for recognizing some of the more common types of tile and patterns. (See Figure 24.) The common types of trim are illustrated in Figure 25.

Tile on countertops may also be trimmed with wood, although the presence of water necessitates frequent refinishing. Make sure to flush the tile out against the wood trim, which is installed first. Silicone or epoxy grout should be used to prevent cracking.

Make sure when grouting tile that a matching or blending color is used. Grout is available in white and in dark colors. A grout of the same color as the tile or a blending shade will make the floor look smoother and the room look larger.

Figure 24. Tile patterns and styles

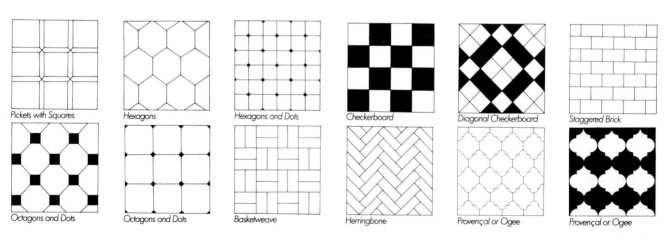

Pickets with Squares   Hexagons   Hexagons and Dots   Checkerboard   Diagonal Checkerboard   Staggered Brick

Octagons and Dots   Octagons and Dots   Basketweave   Herringbone   Provençal or Ogee   Provençal or Ogee

Courtesy Tile Council of America, Inc.

WHAT STYLE OF TILE?

As there are no hard and fast rules in home furnishings, there are none on the use of ceramic tile. Just as an antique Oriental rug can be set exquisitely in contemporary surroundings, so can any tile you like work for you in any room. Featured below are some guidelines from the Tile Council of America, Inc., to get you thinking about styles of tile.

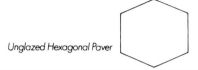

Unglazed Hexagonal Paver

French Country

Floors of hexagonal, unglazed pavers in earthtones enhance typically French floral prints on walls and upholstery, as well as cherry and oak woods in living rooms and bedrooms.

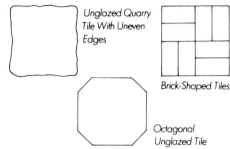

Unglazed Quarry Tile With Uneven Edges

Brick-Shaped Tiles

Octagonal Unglazed Tile

American Country

Unglazed 6x6 or 8x8- inch quarry tile with deliberately uneven edges as flooring, table and counter tops sets off redware collections, quilts, braided rugs, Windsor chairs or painted chests.

Brick-shaped tiles on walls create a hearth-like backdrop for tinware and pewter, decoys and homespun upholstery fabric.

Eight-inch octagonal unglazed tiles in light earthtones, reminiscent of searing sun and sand in the Southwest, are perfect partners to Navajo rugs, painted pottery, Kachina dolls and cactus.

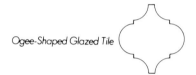

Glazed Tile With Irregular Surface

English

Highboys, Jacobean prints and chintz cabbage roses are at home with square glazed tiles featuring irregular surfaces, in such colors as amber, camel and mushroom.

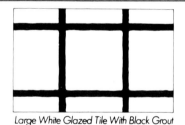

Ogee-Shaped Glazed Tile

Spanish

Ogee-shaped lemon and gold tone tiles combine comfortably with Spanish stucco, bright textiles and dark-stained oak.

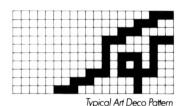

Large White Glazed Tile With Black Grout

Contemporary

Simple floor statements of 8x8-inch white glazed tiles with black grout, and matte finished black or gray-and-white checkerboard patterns maintain the mood of today's micro blinds, state-of-the-art media room equipment and streamlined leather sofas.

Typical Art Deco Pattern

Art Deco

In keeping with this symmetrical, rectilinear, classical style, first popular some 60 years ago, a vast stretch of white glazed wall and floor tile would appropriately be laced with cubist geometric patterns as seen in the shapes of Lalique glassware, Ruhlman furniture and Brandt ironwork.

Decorative Glazed Tile

Faux Marble Tile

Traditional

Decorative glazed tiles for a fireplace that pick up an accent color; borders of matte finish tiles installed around carpeting in living room or den and hallways tiled in *faux* marble or delicate pastel-colored pavers introduce special custom decorating excitement to today's traditionally styled homes.

Figure 25. Types of tile trim

TILE TRIM

The purpose of tile trim is to give an installation a finished look. And, according to the Tile Council of America, Inc., American manufacturers produce the widest selection of trim for every installation. Note that tiles can be set on thin or thick beds of mortar; the silhouette of trim pieces will reflect the difference. Illustrated below are some examples.

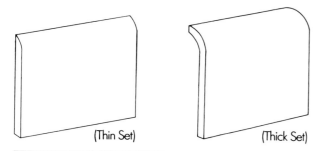

(Thin Set) (Thick Set)

Bullnose

This trim piece is used to finish a tiled area with a rounded edge, at the top of wainscoting, to give a custom look where the tile meets the wall, or around a kitchen sink, for example.

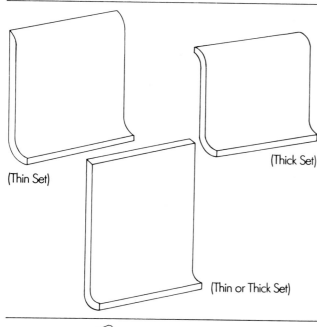

(Thin Set) (Thick Set)

Cove Base

A combination of bullnose and cove tiles, this trim piece is especially appropriate for a flooring installation where wall tiles will not be used. The round top provides a finished transition between flooring and wall covering as well as the easy-to-clean concave feature of the cove tile.

(Thin or Thick Set)

Cove

Installed at the intersection of wall and floor, the smooth, rounded transition piece makes this 90-degree angle easy to clean.

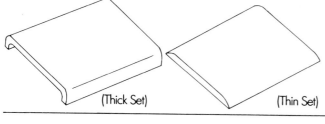

(Thick Set) (Thin Set)

Curb

This piece is used to cover the curb of the shower stall. It offers the finish of a bullnose tile on either side.

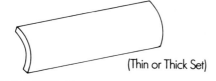

(Thin or Thick Set)

Bead

A rounded piece of tile, usually 4¼ to 6-inches long, similar to a quarter-round piece of wood moulding. The bead can be used horizontally, instead of a bullnose trim piece, to finish a wall installation or vertically as corner trim.

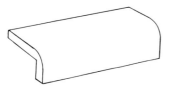

Counter Trim

This piece is used to finish the edge of a ceramic tile counter, vanity or table top.

Courtesy Tile Council of America, Inc.

Wood

Paneling and wooden floors were widely used in the late 19th and early 20th centuries, and a look at the Victorian houses in many cities shows how attractive wood is. And these were built in a time before polyurethane made waterproofing of wood surfaces possible.

Wooden wainscots and floors make a handsome bathroom with contemporary fixtures. The labor involved in finishing wood, however, makes it too expensive for the average home.

One of the largest suppliers of parquet and decorative wood floorings does not recommend its products for baths because of the potential for water damage. Properly finished and cared for, however, wood will serve as well today as it has in the past. (Although not everyone is willing or able to take care of it properly.) Manufacturers recommend that four coats of polyurethane be used on the wood to seal it. A 4-millimeter polyethylene vapor barrier should be used behind the wood, and rustproof nails must be used. All wood should be kiln-dried to a moisture content of 6 to 12 percent. Moisture content above 12 percent usually results in nail pops, warping, shrinkage, and cracking.

Wood paneling comes prefinished in various grades. Such products as wood veneers over plywood or hardboard, printed wood grains on vinyl, and plastic laminates all should be checked to see if they are recommended by the manufacturer for bathrooms. Durability and resistance to moisture and stains vary.

Wood flooring is available in strips or parquetry. Oak floors that are properly maintained are almost as durable as tile. Parquet wood blocks are usually 12 inches × 12 inches and installed much like vinyl tile. They are sold finished or unfinished.

Marble

Marble makes a handsome bath countertop, but its expense reserves it for the custom home. Although it is extremely durable, marble is subject to staining and abrasion, especially in white and light-colored shades. Marble must be sealed to prevent water absorption.

Marble comes in slabs and must be installed by a specialist. Also available are marble tiles, used the same way as other tiles. Avoid using marble for floors because it is very slippery, especially when wet.

Granite

Granite is an attractive but expensive and heavy stone. It is not as prone to staining and abrasion as marble. Available in slabs and tiles, granite requires a specialist for installation. Granite is available in colors ranging from pale off-whites to mottled effects and darker tones.

Cultured Marble and Onyx

Cultured marble and onyx are actually cast polyester resin; in the case of marble, this is filled with crushed marble. The material is molded and then cut and polished. It's water resistant, lightweight, and relatively inexpensive. Suitable for countertops, this man-made stone weighs much less than the real thing. Translucent onyx designs are more expensive than opaque ones but have exceptional sales appeal; they are primarily used for lavatories and countertops.

Solid Plastics

DuPont introduced solid plastics with their cast acrylic, Corian®. The material's color is solid throughout, it has no grout lines, is exceptionally durable, does not readily stain, and damage can be scoured or sanded out. Although generally used for countertops and walls, it is sometimes used for fixtures. Available in sheets, integral vanity tops and lavatories, molded lavatories, and tub tops, cast acrylic is excellent for walls and surrounds (Figure 26). Decorative edges are available also.

Cast acrylic is generally available in various thicknesses: ¼ inch, 5/16 inch, ½ inch, and ¾ inch. The ¼ inch or 5/16 inch size is used for walls, tub surrounds, and showers; the other sizes are used for countertops and partitions.

Cast polyesters, another type of solid plastic, are nonporous, eliminating the need for a gel coat, which means matt and textured finishes are now available. The new generation of cultured marble and onyx are made of cast polyester. They are stain and acid resistant; burns can be sanded off, and nicks can be repaired with a special patch kit. The color is solid, and they can be cut, routed, shaped, drilled, and sanded like wood, then polished to a high gloss. Seams are almost invisible. The trade names for these materials are Avonite®, Formica 2000X®, and Perma-Bilt's Marlan. (See Figure 27.) These are usually available in standard 3-foot × 10-foot × ½-inch sheets.

The American National Standards Institute certifies the quality of these materials. If such a product carries a label certifying the ANSI standard, it has been tested for surface abrasions, structural integrity, wear, cleanability, flammability, resistance to stains and cigarette burns, and changes to water temperature. In addition, drain fitting connections are tested, loads are placed on lavatory tops, and stress points are inspected (Maass 1987).

Another program that assures buyers that a manufacturer is using the best available new technology and materials is sponsored by the Cultured Marble Institute and the National Association of Home Builders National Research Center (Maass 1987).

Laminates

Since laminates were introduced in the 1920s, they have proven their worth in millions of homes. Durable, water- and stain-resistant, they are now made in solid color sheets, which eliminate grout lines. (See Figure 28.) Formica®, Wilsonart®, and Nevamar® are well-known brands.

Post-formed laminated tops have curved backsplashes and front edges, are sold in stock lengths, and priced by the running foot. These may be difficult to handle in corners and cannot be cut to narrower widths or in irregular shapes.

Laminates come in a wide range of colors, textures, and finishes. The new, color-through laminate edgings eliminate unsightly grout lines and also perform better. Since the color is solid, nicks and chips do not show, and edges stay new looking for years. These laminates may be routed or sandblasted. Manufacturers' instructions, including use of the recommended adhesive, should be followed carefully.

Laminates come in a ⅟₁₆-inch thickness for countertops; a ⅓-inch thickness can be used for walls and surrounds. Standard widths are 24 inches, 30 inches, 36 inches, and 48 inches, in lengths from 4 to 12 feet.

Paint and Wallpaper

The development of drywall specially made for areas with high humidity (called greenwall) has alleviated problems with painted surfaces in bathrooms. Greenwall, which is made of specially treated paper, is simpler to prime and seal than regular drywall.

In bathrooms, either drywall or greenwall must be primed and sealed with an alkyd interior primer/sealer that is insensitive to water and humidity and gives the extra protection necessary. Primer or sealer raises a light fuzz on the wall surface of conventional drywall, so sanding is required. (Wallpaper, however, may be applied right over drywall.) Corner and ceiling caulking is crucial to prevent humidity from getting behind the walls, where it can cause rot.

Latex paints are water based and water soluble. They dry quickly and wash easily. Semi- or high-gloss latex may be used in baths, except for the shower area.

Alkyd paints have as a base such oils as soya, safflower, or linseed (which yellows faster than the others). They are soluble in petroleum-based solvents or thinners. Their resistance to moisture makes them a good choice for baths, and they should be used in shower areas.

A small amount of wallpaper in a bath can make a big difference in aesthetics. Paper should be fabric or vinyl backed, washable, and strippable. Apply with high-humidity pastes.

Mirrors

Adding a mirrored wall gives the illusion of space and adds a fashion look (Figure 29). Mirrors should be placed as a matter of course over vanities.

Mirrors on walls beside tubs, on closet doors, and used in other creative ways add to the sales appeal of the room, as well. Mirrors facing garden walls will bring the outdoors inside, for instance.

Mirrors adjacent to showers will tend to fog, so placement in the dressing area is preferable.

Carpeting

A luxurious floor covering for a bath, carpeting visually expands the room when it flows from there into the bedroom. It should not, however, extend into the tub and shower area or be used for the tub surrounds, unless the buyer so specifies, because it will be damaged by exposure to water.

Regular carpeting retains moisture and encourages bacteria growth. If using carpet, select one that is resistant to mildew, stain, and odors. (Indoor-outdoor carpeting is not luxurious looking or feeling; its use should be restricted to the outdoors.)

Figure 26. Corian® countertops and tub surrounds exemplify the versatility of the new bathroom materials available.

Courtesy DuPont

Figure 27. A cultured marble tub surrounds blends the beauty of stone with practicality of installation and use.

Courtesy Avonite®

Figure 28. Laminated countertops are popular and good-looking.

Courtesy Nevamar®

Figure 29. Mirrored walls extend the bath and create the illusion of great depth.

Courtesy Wood-Mode Cabinetry

Resilient Flooring

Resilient floorings (Figure 30) are handsome and practical, water and stain resistent, and available in a wide variety of colors and patterns to fit any decorative theme.

Vinyl tiles come in 9-inch × 9-inch and 12-inch × 12-inch squares. They are either inlaid or printed and may have a clear urethane or vinyl top layer.

Vinyl sheet goods come in rolls 6- or 12-feet wide. Generally, sheet flooring has moisture-proof backing and a no-wax finish. Sheeting may be rotovinyl, with the pattern printed or in inlaid vinyl. Either type is protected with a clear urethane or vinyl top layer. The inlaid type

Figure 30. Resilient flooring

Courtesy Armstrong

has greater depth of color and higher resistance to tearing and punching. No-wax finishes are either urethane or vinyl. The urethane is tougher than the vinyl and keeps its finish longer.

The newer, stretchable-backed floorings can be installed with fastenings only along the edges. This helps them cover minor irregularities in the sub-floor.

Ceilings

Ceilings may be painted or papered, just as walls are, or made of exotic materials, including wood.

Ceiling tiles can also be used. They should be washable: regular acoustical tile is too absorbent for use in a bathroom.

Panel or tile suspended ceilings can also be used.

Achieve a dramatic effect with concealed lighting behind suspended ceilings and with strategically placed spots recessed in the ceiling. Think of the ceiling as a decorative element: it can add drama, provide a sense of space, and be a source of light. Opening up the ceiling and using beams as plant shelves in the soaring space doubles the apparent size of a small room by carrying the eye upward. A skylight in the ceiling floods the room with light and enhances its appearance, as well as its practicality. (See Chapter 6 for more information on skylights in baths.)

Chapter 6

Lighting, Heating, Ventilation, and Insulation

Lighting

As the bath has changed from a 5-foot × 7-foot white cell to a retreat and a bathing room that is an extension of the bedroom, its lighting has evolved to more than an incandescent bulb or two. Light is an integral part of the overall ambience of a room, and its proper use can make or break the decor.

Light sources have become part of the architectural plan. Is the room windowless, on the inside of the home? If so, how can it be lighted? Is it located on the outside? Then how can the windows be sheltered from prying eyes? These and other lighting subjects are considered in the following paragraphs.

Natural Light

A foremost consideration in planning for lighting is natural light. As many rooms as possible should have a source of natural light, so they can be enjoyed during the day without artificial illumination.

Recognizing that the siting of the house affects the amount and type of light that is distributed throughout is the first step in planning. If the bedroom/bath is on the eastern side, it gets the morning sun. If it's on the western side, it gets the late afternoon sun. In either case, the sunlight hits the windows at different angles in summer and winter.

The summer light hits at a different angle than does the winter light (Figure 31). In winter the light is more nearly parallel to the earth and hits more directly. If snow or sand is on the ground, the reflection from these adds to the glare. This also generates heat. Guard against great expanses of glass on a southern exposure that will get the direct light of a winter sun.

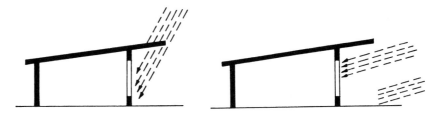

Figure 31. Angles of the sun in summer and winter affect the heat and light in a room.

Courtesy National Kitchen and Bath Association

Figure 32. Dramatic windows flood these baths with light.

Courtesy Owens Corning

Courtesy Villeroy and Boch

Builders 100 years ago understood how to increase the amount of natural light. They installed movable glass transoms over interior doors, helping light flow through the house, as well as providing a source of ventilation. Builders today are using similar devices in the walls between bathroom and bedroom, admitting light and allowing for privacy.

The skylight is another feature Victorian-era builders used to flood interior rooms with natural light. A bathroom skylight was preferred by 49 percent of the respondents to one study of consumer tastes (National Association of Home Builders 1985). The work of some of the foremost interior designers and architects today shows they are well aware of this. Skylights are being incorporated in all types of architecture.

In addition to modern adaptations of transoms and skylights, clerestory windows, glass block walls, garden windows, and dramatically shaped windows are providing bathrooms with precious light, making them seem larger, more elegant, and adding to their sales appeal (Figure 32).

The beauty of skylights and clerestory windows in place of conventional windows is not only the feeling of openness that they impart but also the extra wall space left available for closets, storage, and furniture.

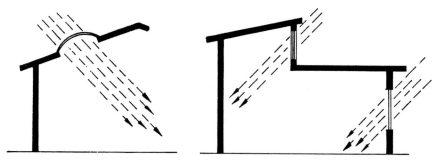

Figure 33. The placement of the windows and the angle of the roofline determine how much direct sun reaches a room.

Courtesy National Kitchen and Bath Association

In estimating the effectiveness of a skylight, calculate that each square foot of the skylight illuminates approximately 2 square feet of room. Thus, if a room design includes a whirlpool, the skylight can be sized and positioned to surround the area with light, creating a dramatic setting.

Consider the position of the sun in relation to the house in your planning. For instance, southern-exposure windows or clerestories provide sunlight most of the day, while northern-exposure windows provide light but practically no sun. The path of the light can be figured from the configuration of the roofline and the skylight or clerestory windows, as shown in Figure 33.

Figure 34. A glass block wall sheds diffused light over the lavatory and increases the sense of space created by mirrored walls.

Courtesy DuPont

Direct sunlight, however, streaming through a skylight or clerestory window can be harsh and glaring. Diffuser panels can mitigate this, as can properly placed plants. By positioning the light source on a northern exposure, light will come in evenly all day without sharp contrasts and the heat of direct sunlight.

In addition, a skylight placed on a flat roof or one getting the afternoon sun in a hot climate can raise the temperature to an uncomfortable and wasteful level.

Adding a window wall facing a courtyard or garden is another device to expand the entire room, as well as provide additional light. Glass block on the window will diffuse light over the tub and the room while providing needed privacy. (See Figure 34.)

Artificial Light

Artificial light may be either incandescent or fluorescent.

Incandescent lights provide warmth, as well as bright spots of light, that are usually warm and flattering in tone. The oldest source of electric light, they consume more power and generate more heat than fluorescent tubes, but they have many advantages, besides being flattering. Bulbs are interchangeable, light can be directed to a specific surface, and fixtures are generally easier and less expensive to install. Incandescent lights can be recessed, surface mounted, or suspended and lend themselves to a wide variety of interior styles.

Fluorescent lights yield three to five times as much light per watt as incandescents, and they generate little heat. (See Appendix 3 for a comparison of the efficiency of fluorescent and incandescent lighting.) Many associate fluorescent lighting with the glaring, unflattering lights found in commercial establishments. Actually, they come in several types, ranging from cold to warm tones.

Fluorescent lights blend well with incandescent, and both may be used in a room. It is important to determine what type of light is best for the room. A warm light may make a cool white room look grey. A cool white or deluxe cool white should be used in this case. Check a color scheme under various lights to find the best ones. (See Appendix 3 for details on selecting fluorescent lighting.)

Many fluorescent lights are utilitarian looking, so they may need to be concealed by soffits, valances, or behind tray or dropped ceilings.

The Uses of Bathroom Lighting

Bathroom lighting consists of task light, general light, and mood light. Consider all three of these in creating attractive, appealing baths.

Task light is that which is directed toward the performance of a special activity, such as shaving. Task light should provide shadow-free illumination for shaving, make-up application, and other grooming tasks. This includes shower lights bright enough for shaving and bathing.

The greatest problems with task light are glare and shadows. An overhead light produces a shadow on the face.

Light flowing from the sides of a mirror eliminates shadows. If using a theatrical lighting arrangement (small bulbs along the rim of a mirror) for this effect, the mirror must be at least 30 inches wide, so the bulbs don't shine directly into the user's eye. Light from below or above a mirror can also provide an efficient source of task light. Soffit lighting is desirable.

General lighting is the background lighting that bathes the entire room, enhancing it, as well as providing practical illumination. It reduces the contrast between the task-lighted areas and the remainder of the room, providing shadow-free, relatively uniform light. In the bedroom and bath area, it should be bright enough to light up corners, drawers, and cabinets to permit general use of the rooms.

General lighting in the bathroom should be provided by natural, as well as artificial sources. If the room has windows of any kind, it may not need additional light during the day. The amount of light provided should be based on night use and can be determined by the square footage of surface to be lighted. (See Appendix 3 for general lighting requirements.)

Darkly painted or paneled rooms require more wattage because dark color absorbs light, so wattage must be increased accordingly. Avoid dimly lit bathrooms, which turn buyers off.

General lighting can be provided by a variety of methods. Wall fixtures may provide task lighting with mirrors, in addition to general light. Ceiling fixtures may vary from chandeliers to track lights, high hats, and eyeballs. Architectural lighting includes coves, valances, and cornices. Tray and dropped ceilings are additional possibilities.

Dressing rooms and closets adjacent to bathrooms should be kept in mind when planning the lighting.

Mood lighting provides the glamor that stimulates sales appeal.

Dimmer switches are an inexpensive way to create eye-appeal. Use them to highlight a whirlpool in a prominent position in the room. A dimmer on theatrical lighting around a vanity mirror reduces glare when the mirror is being used for dressing, rather than for make-up application.

Any special bath feature should be emphasized with lights: spot lights for plants, floodlights for a private garden, special lights for a fireplace are all effective.

In showing a home, mood lights are welcoming lights. Switch on the task lights to demonstrate how practical each room is, then turn them off.

Heating

Despite the efficiency of today's heating systems, bathrooms often require additional heat. Although a room may be comfortable normally, when the body is wet, the air seems chilly. Using a whirlpool in an open space can make this problem even more pronounced.

In the winter or in homes where the nighttime temperature is set back, it is also important to be able to heat the bathroom quickly for early morning showers.

Auxiliary heating units are the answer and are available separately or in combination with fans and lights. They require a separate switch and circuit. When combination units are installed, each function should have its own switch. Two commonly used auxiliary heating units are infra-red lamps and electric heaters.

Infra-red lamps may be recessed in the wall or ceiling or surface mounted. They are silent, swift, and energy efficient; the radiant heat warms the body, not the air. These may be the ideal solution for tubs placed in open areas.

Electric heaters are available for wall or ceiling mounting and have fan-forced heat. They are fast and adjustable and available in combination with fans and/or lights. They must have thermostats. (See the next section in this chapter.)

Ventilation

Too often sumptuous bathrooms, as well as modest ones, are inadequately ventilated. This is not only uncomfortable for the user when bathroom humidity likens it to a steam bath, but it can damage the home. Excess humidity will crack and peel paint, warp doors, rust metal, cause joist and framing deterioration, promote mildew, and make maintenance difficult.

All of these problems can be prevented with an exhaust fan. The Home Ventilating Institute (HVI) recommends fans capable of changing the air at least eight times per hour. Fans are rated on how much cubic feet of air they move per minute (CFM). Ratings are found on unit labels, manufacturers' brochures, and in the HVI Certified Home Ventilating Products Directory.

In addition, exhaust fans should be quiet, with a sone (measurement of sound) level as close to 1.5 as possible. Fans with sensor controls or automatic timers are preferable to prevent excess usage. (For details on how to determine a fan's CFM and sone rating, see Appendix 3.)

Insulation and Noise Control

One of the most objectionable features in new homes is inadequate insulation for noise control in the bath. In multifamily dwellings, this can be a serious problem. In single-family homes, it can be a major drawback but one that is easily remedied with planning.

Preliminary planning and common sense can eliminate or at least minimize the need for special techniques (which may be costly) to control sound. In general, follow a few simple principles:

- Locate rooms for gatherings as far from noise sources as possible.
- Segregate noisy rooms from quiet ones.
- Isolate and/or reduce noise sources.
- Use space as a buffer.
- Avoid air paths between rooms.
- Choose quiet appliances and equipment.
- Use staggered stud construction.
- Avoid mounting fixtures or cabinets on the resilient channel side of the wall; mount on staggered studs.
- Place wall fixtures 24 inches apart on opposite sides of the walls.
- In staggered-stud walls, allow 24 inches of horizontal distance between switches and outlets. Do not locate a switch and outlet in the same stud space.
- Seal cracks and holes. Use resilient, nonhardening caulking at floor and ceiling of all partitions and around electrical outlets and plumbing and other openings.

Although these design principles are the main methods for isolating sound, acoustical materials absorb sound and additionally reduce the sound level in rooms where they are used. (See Appendix 3 for further information on insulation.)

Chapter 7

Storage

Home buyers today want a bathroom that has ample storage space for everything from towels to make-up. Almost 81 percent of consumers responding to a survey stated that they wanted linen cabinets in their bathrooms (*Builder* 1986).

A storage wall provides soundproofing and serves as a room divider. Storage can be built around lavatories, above a wide ledge by a tub, or suspended over a water closet: with a little ingenuity, extra bathroom storage can be built in.

In most cases cabinets can provide such storage. The handsome cabinetry available today makes designing storage simpler. Many manufacturers now have products that are adaptable to the bath and bedroom, as well as the kitchen.

Look for built-in wardrobes, vanity cabinets with pull-out drawers for bottle storage, pull-out hampers, corner wall units, pull-out ironing boards, sliding trays, and medicine chests to match other cabinets (Figure 35). Shallow cabinets, sewing machine bases, and various shelf units add to the options available.

Bathroom vanities require a shallow drawer for small items, in addition to a deep one to handle bottles of all sizes. Storage for cleaning materials should be provided. Shelving for towels and sheets will not

Figure 35. Built-in compartments add compact storage and sales appeal.

Courtesy Poggenpohl

accommodate blankets, which need a deeper space. (Open shelves are great for decorations and towels, but every bath needs closed cabinets.)

Dressing rooms or areas next to baths should be planned to accommodate female and male wardrobes and accessories. Large vanities adjacent to the dressing room provide storage for lingerie, sweaters, and other clothing. Such planning is especially important when square footage from the bedroom has been added to the bath.

A fold-away ironing board in the dressing room is a desirable feature. A complete workroom (Figure 36) is even better, when space permits. The most convenient location for a washer/dryer and ironing board is near the bedrooms because the major part of the laundry is generated in the bedrooms and baths.

The bath shown in Figure 37 is an excellent example of a lavish bath with well-planned storage. The lavatory is at one end of a grooming center with drawers of various sizes to accommodate tall bottles, as well as lingerie. The linen storage has both deep and shallow spaces for towels, washcloths, and bed linens. The other grooming center provides a smaller array of drawers for the male. Elements from this bath can be adapted for smaller baths.

Storage presents a greater problem in smaller, less luxurious baths, but providing it is vital. In small areas the most obvious place to do this is around the lavatory. Vanities that stretch from wall to wall offer a good source of storage space.

Offsetting the lavatory in the countertop can increase the amount of cabinet space underneath. Allow for a run of cabinets that extend up a wall or are suspended over the vanity top. Space for at least a 30-inch-wide mirror should be provided over the lavatory. Thus, a vanity wall 60 inches long allows space for a mirror and a shallow cabinet or open shelves sharing the wall above the vanity top. Make sure to balance the elements well. (Since sidelights require a minimum of 30 inches between them to prevent glare, an arrangement of this type also requires lighting from above and below.)

The elevation in Figure 38 shows how a tub/shower unit can be framed with storage. This bath has a make-up bar on one side of the tub, with a storage unit on the other, which balances the arrangement. The closet area is 39 inches wide, the make-up bar is 44 inches wide, and the overall effect is pleasing.

This bath also has two lavatories, a toilet, and bidet. The wall space above the toilet and bidet holds shallow cupboards, and both the his and her lavatories have vanity storage.

The space in this 156-inch × 109-inch (16 feet × 9 feet) room is used to its fullest (Figure 38). Two can use it at once; it has more privacy than would an open arrangement; and it has storage for linens, make-up, and sundries, as well as cleaning materials. Select ideas from this bath to adapt for smaller rooms. The space around the toilet is especially well used and can also work in a more restricted space.

Another clever use of space provides a compartment for the water closet and extra pull-out storage compartments for shampoos, hair dryers, and other sundries. The cabinet space above the storage walls can be used for linen storage. The angled mirrors increase the usefulness of the area for dressing.

On the opposite wall, the cabinet contains a hamper, as well as plentiful storage space. Ceiling spots dramatize the tub and vanity areas.

Figure 36. A complete laundry room adjacent to the bedrooms provides storage.

Courtesy Wood-Mode Cabinetry

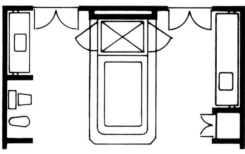

Figure 37. This luxury bath provides plenty of storage space.

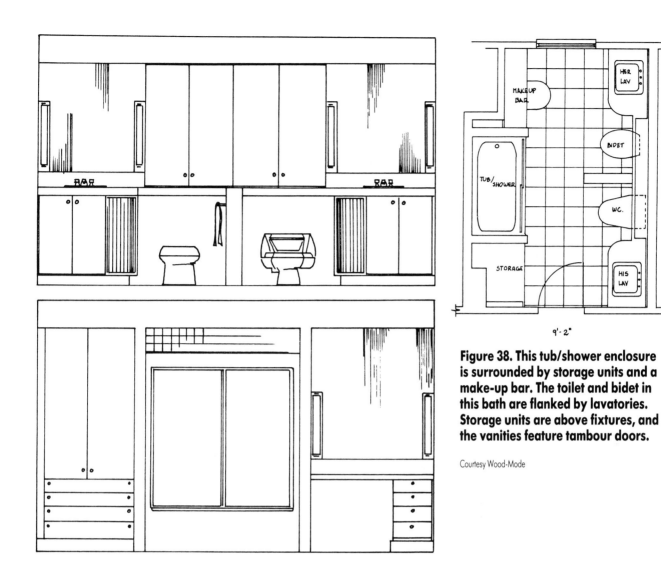

Figure 38. This tub/shower enclosure is surrounded by storage units and a make-up bar. The toilet and bidet in this bath are flanked by lavatories. Storage units are above fixtures, and the vanities feature tambour doors.

Courtesy Wood-Mode

Use Walls for Storage

Wall space is a virtue in a living room or dining room. Bedrooms need enough wall space for beds, chests, and other furniture. But in dressing rooms and baths, blank wall space is useless.

Blank walls can be turned into useful storage. Shallow cabinets 4 to 9 inches deep are one solution, when space is at a premium.

Deepening walls to turn them into closets and mirroring closet doors make the room look larger, while providing soundproofing and useful storage. If space is scarce, bifold or sliding mirror doors may be the answer. Space saved this way can be used for a dressing area, leaving a usable wall in the bedroom. If space is too shallow for this plan, place shelves or cabinets between the studs to gain extra space. Make sure to place these against a sound barrier.

Euro-style Versus Traditional Cabinet Construction

When space is tight, frameless, Euro-style cabinets save needed inches and make space more accessible. Euro-style cabinets may have specially designed drawers with shallow and deep storage space and offer a wide variety of choices. Although generally thought of as a contemporary design, traditional door styles are available.

The traditional method of cabinet construction in the United States, face-frame construction, is still the most widely used. In this construction, the cabinet is framed in, and the door is then affixed. A wider range of cabinet styles can be found in this construction than is available in Euro-style.

The combination of open shelving and cabinets dresses up a room (Figure 39). Open shelving can also be used as a room divider to separate the dressing area.

Figure 39. Euro-style cabinets combine with open shelving to create useful and decorative storage that highlights a centered whirlpool. Note how the mirrored wall increases the sense of space.

Courtesy St. Charles Cabinets and Whirlpool

Cabinet Materials

Wood is still the predominant material used for cabinets, and it gives a warm feeling to any room. Wooden cabinets come in styles suitable for any type of decor, from colonial to contemporary. They can be starkly smooth and elegant or handsomely carved.

The deep richness of mahogany, the soft lightness of pine, painted surfaces: all of these exemplify the versatility of wood.

Generally, wooden cabinets are topped with laminates or other durable materials that withstand water and moisture.

As shown in the bath in Figure 37, laminates provide color, good-looking shapes, and a look of luxury. Surfaces and cabinet faces can be blended. A sweep of color and the use of a single material add a sense of space to the room.

Laminates come in an enormous variety of colors and finishes, which makes them easily adaptable to any decorative theme, from traditional to Art Deco and contemporary.

Laminates and other man-made materials are durable, easy to maintain, and ideal for use in the steamy atmosphere of a bath. A judicious combination of materials can save money, while providing an upscale look. For instance, a high-quality countertop with custom edges on a standard vanity base can upgrade the entire room; and combining tile and carpeting on the floor answers the consumer preference for a floor that is not completely tiled.

Space-expanding Ideas

In addition to shallow cabinets and cabinets for special uses, consider the following methods to gain storage space:

- Recess mirrored medicine chests to flank a large mirror over vanities. (A 14-inch cabinet fits between 16-inch on center studs.)
- Shrink vanity area to install a storage unit beside it.
- Use wire storage shelves on doors and roll-out shelves in vanities.
- Offset lavatories to allow for adjacent pull-out shelving and other storage.
- Run narrow banjo shelves over water closets. Add shallow cabinet or open shelves above. (Leave at least 12 inches of space to allow for servicing the flush tank.)
- Recess areas between studs for paper holder and narrow shelves, using a door on those for cleaners and toilet brush.
- Build a make-up bar 14 inches wide, the best depth for practical use and a space-saving device. A narrow bench fits well in this space.
- Extend the tub surrounds to provide shelf space for decorative and useful items at one end or side. Adding an extra 6 to 10 inches to the length of a tub enclosure yields a luxury look.
- Stretch a vanity wall across a corner and extend a narrow top along the side walls with shallow cabinets beneath to add storage and eye appeal.
- Provide shelves at the foot of a tub for storage of shampoos, soaps, bath oils, and other items stored in waterproof containers. Tub surrounds can be designed so that such shelves are placed between the studs.

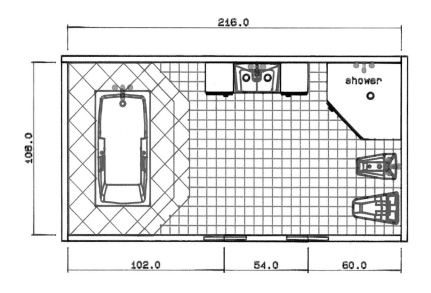

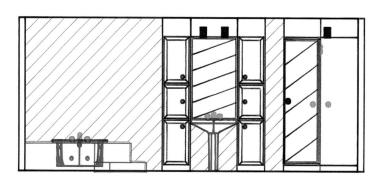

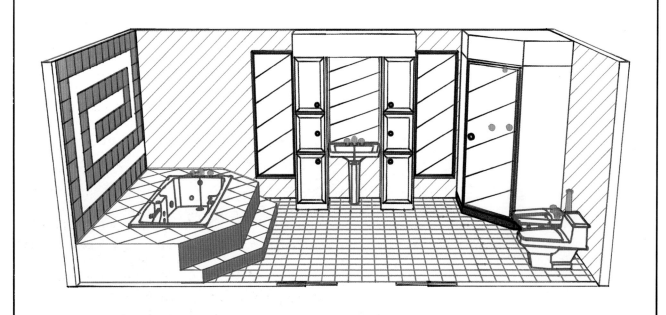

Chapter 8

How to Design a Bathroom

Good design achieves a balance among all the elements that must go into a bathroom. Since money and, consequently, space are generally the controlling factors in design, the end result is usually a trade-off between the ultimate desired and the ultimate affordable.

The challenge lies in finding the balance. The interior designer is a key player and should be brought into the picture in the beginning. The designer can work with the architect or the builder to make any structural changes that are desirable before construction begins.

Help With Bathroom Design

An increasing number of designers are specializing in kitchen and bath design. The National Kitchen and Bath Association (NKBA) has developed a rigorous program for kitchen designers. Those who complete it successfully become Certified Kitchen Designers and use "CKD" after their names. The NKBA sponsors educational programs for bath design and will soon launch a formal certification program like the one for kitchen designers.

The American Society of Interior Designers (ASID) offers professional know-how. Members must meet tough standards to belong. To learn the names of members, contact local chapters, or write to their national headquarters at 1430 Broadway, New York, New York 10018.

Preparing elevations to show what a room will look like with cabinets, fixtures, and accessories, such as lights and mirrors, is a time-consuming job requiring the professional training of an interior designer or architectural draftsman. Such techniques may be a luxury for a builder doing his own plans. The latest and most exciting development in bath design is the use of computer assisted design (CAD) software, which executes plans in a few hours. A sophisticated program that prepares floor plans, elevations, perspectives, and shows the plans in detailed computer-generated drawings (Figure 40) has been developed by American Standard Plumbing Products. (It also lists products and costs.) Builders, designers, architects, and plumbing contractors can use this service at no charge through American Standard's district office at 50 W. 40th Street, New York, New York, 10018, or in showrooms in Pittsburgh, Chicago, Dallas, and Los Angeles.

With this system the computer executes an efficient plan that shows exactly what the bath will look like. (See other examples of these

Figure 40. CAD drawings of elevations, perspectives, and floor plans show how a bath will look when finished.

Courtesy American Standard

drawings in Chapters 9 and 10.) A rough sketch is transformed into a professional layout, and routine baths are redesigned to make maximum use of space for the ultimate in sales appeal.

In addition, Eljer Plumbing has developed a professional design program using computer assistance that is available in 300 showrooms and other locations. This provides finished floor plans, elevations, and perspective drawings. Eljer has gone so far as to provide a material board, including swatches and color recommendations.

Principles of Bath Design

A sound understanding of the elements and principles of bathroom design enables you to design better baths, evaluate the designs of others, and work more efficiently with home buyers. Often it is the rearrangement of the room, the addition of architectural elements, such as skylights, or even an extra square foot or the upgrading of the fixtures and fittings that make the difference between a bath with sales appeal and one without. The following is a list of considerations to keep in mind when designing a bath:

- Know the market
- Determine the most convenient location
- Select the proper fixtures
- Select the most useful, handsome fittings
- Provide adequate lighting and ventilation
- Provide auxiliary heating
- Install the right insulation
- Include useful, spacious storage
- Place fixtures optimally
- Use appealing aesthetics for color/texture/mood

Since homes are designed for selected market segments, it is imperative to have a specific buyer profile in mind when designing the bath. Designing a luxury master bath and a minimal second bath in a home for a family with two school-age children is as off-target as putting a basic bathroom in a luxury empty-nester home.

After determining the market, you must decide how many fixtures to put in each bath. Consider the master bath first, which should have the highest-quality fixtures possible. A whirlpool should be a primary consideration for the master bath. This bath, however, can be sold as an upgrade option, building flexibility into the room.

The master bath should be designed with two working people in mind. Compartments, toilet areas that are closed off for privacy, lavatories that can be used simultaneously by two people or used when one person is in the shower—all these devices make the bath a versatile, two-person room.

Simply placing a lavatory in the bedroom is not the answer. Nor is arbitrarily positioning a fixture into a nook. For instance, if there isn't enough room for someone to pass behind another standing at a lavatory, the bath is not designed for two. It remains a one-person-at-a-time room.

Dressing space, mirrored closet doors, a large, mirrored wall, skylights and/or windows, vanity lights, storage access in the dressing area are all elements to be considered in designing baths with sales appeal. These can often be added to a standard bath to increase its usefulness and apparent size.

The second bath for any household with children should be designed for dual usage. This requires lavatories separated from the main bath, compartmentalized toilets with doors, if possible, and adequate storage space for towels, sheets, blankets, and necessities to serve all but the master bedroom. Storage space that opens into the hallway may be preferable to that opening into the bath itself.

Once you know what type of bath to build, the next step is fitting the fixtures into the allocated space. By laying out the room prior to construction, you can decide whether you need to change the configuration, allow for an additional wet wall, or move the location of one or more baths, walls, or doors. Determining space and layout in the planning stage can save dollars and time and help sales later.

Locate the wet wall or walls. If the house has but one wet wall to serve both kitchen and bath, this governs the placement of all fixtures. If you have the flexibility afforded by two or more plumbing stacks, then placement can be determined based on aesthetics.

Plumbing pipes should be placed in a warm wall to prevent freezing. In northern climates, allow 3½ inches of insulation on the cold side of the pipe, none on the warm side. An insulated 2-inch × 4-inch framed outerwall is insufficient.

The minimum and desirable sizes of fixtures are contained in Table 3:

Table 3. Bathroom Fixture Size in Inches

	Width	Depth	Height
Lavatory			
Minimum	24	21	30
Desirable	36	21	34-36
(Pedestal lavatories are usually 32 inches high.)			
Tub			
Minimum	32	54	16
Desirable	32	60	16
Shower			
Minimum	32	32	76
Desirable	36	48	80
Toilet			
2-piece, close-coupled	21	29	27*
1-piece	21	29	20*

*15″ seat

Table 4. Clearances in the Bathroom in Inches

Area	Minimum Clearance	Desirable Clearance
Behind vanity chair		
To push back	26	36
To allow passage	44	
Lavatory	36	44
Bathing child at tub or adult dressing	30 × 42 (floor area for kneeling/dressing)	
Rowing machines	78 × 48	
Over/under washer/dryer (full size)	28 wide × 28 deep × 74 high (allow ½-1″ all around plus 4″ for plumbing/venting behind)	

Fixture size in addition to the clearance needed govern the layout and room size. The University of Illinois Small Homes Council/Building Research Council has determined proper clearances between fixtures. (See Figures 41 to 44.) Those clearances that meet or exceed these satisfy most or all local building codes. In addition to allowances for fixtures, space must be allowed for use of an appliance or work area. (See Table 4.)

Figure 41. Lavatory clearances

MINIMUM

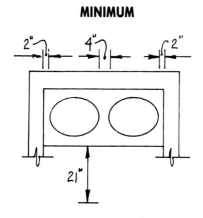

DESIRABLE

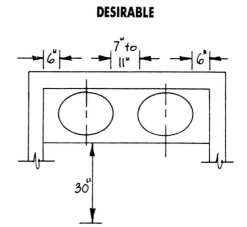

MINIMUM

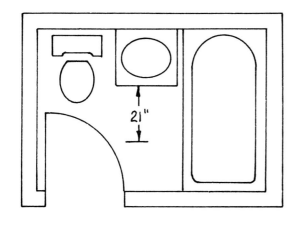

DESIRABLE

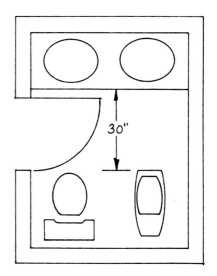

Figure 42. Toilet clearances

MINIMUM

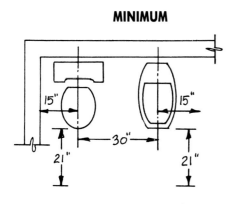

DESIRABLE

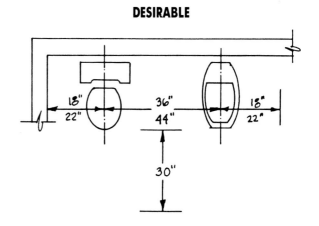

MINIMUM

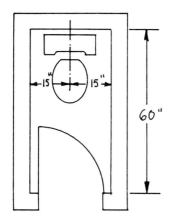

DESIRABLE

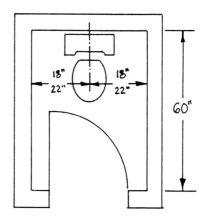

MINIMUM

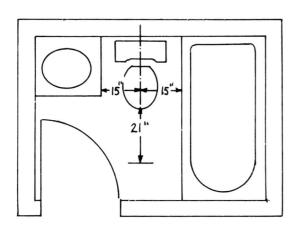

DESIRABLE

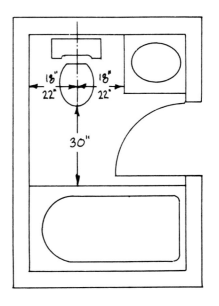

Courtesy National Kitchen and Bath Association

Figure 43. Bathtub clearances

MINIMUM

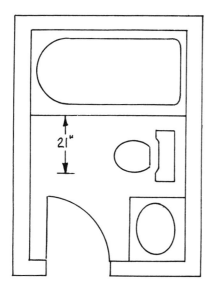

DESIRABLE

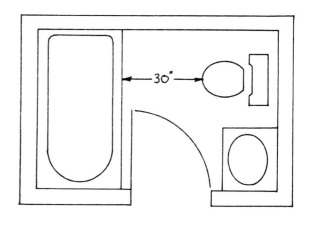

Figure 44. Shower clearances

MINIMUM

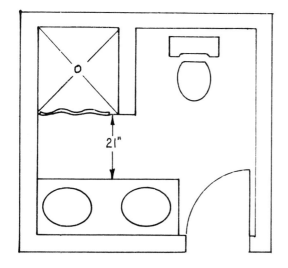

DESIRABLE

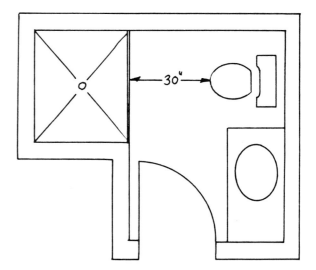

The Floor Plan

The bath is probably the most difficult of all rooms to plan, because it offers so little flexibility. Fixtures must be connected to walls; the economics of additional plumbing walls must be considered, the size and make-up of fixtures preclude a great deal of versatility in layout, and generally, the space available is limited.

But it is possible to overcome all these difficulties by planning ahead. The following pages show various layouts for differently sized baths. These are designed to help in door and fixture placement. Often shifting a door a foot or two, changing the placement of a closet, or moving lavatories from an inside wall to an outside wall can increase the usable floor space in the bath, as well as turn it into a more practical, attractive room.

Figures 45 and 46 show the minimum and desirable space for a one-wall and a two-wall bathroom. Note the dimensions of the space needed for each fixture, the room required for door swing, and the overall square footage.

Study the sample floor plans on the following pages. These plans may apply to baths that range from powder rooms to large, elaborate master baths. The plans give many design ideas.

To design your own bath, begin with your floor plan on the blue print. Use the grid paper provided in Appendix 4 to draw in the bath dimension. Each square on the grid represents one square foot. Indicate doors and windows. A 32-inch door is preferable, and it should swing against a wall or a flat fixture, such as the side of the tub, if it swings in. A door swinging in presents a safety hazard if someone falls against it inside the bath. Doors, however, should not open into a hall or otherwise interfere with traffic or safety.

Consider whether a pocket door might solve any space problems, even though it may be more difficult to open and maintain and less efficient for sound proofing than a conventional door.

Now, using the templates provided in Appendix 4 or those from a supplier, lay the tub, lavatory, and toilet on the floor plan. Using the architectural symbols provided in Appendix 4, position all components. Indicate heaters and fans. If a skylight is part of the plan, check its position in relation to the whirlpool, tub, or vanity area. The skylight should enhance them, if possible, by illuminating the fixtures and area.

After you have sketched in the plan, analyze it for eye appeal and practicality from a plumbing standpoint, as well as from a user's standpoint.

Now is the time to ask yourself whether you can do more to enhance the room's sales appeal:

- Can you add 2 more feet and fit a 72-inch tub in? Can you place the tub on a platform with only one side against a wall?
- Can you compartmentalize the fixtures?
- Can the closet be a baffle wall?
- Do the specifications require triple-glazed glass or low-emissivity plastic layers in the window to keep the room comfortable?
- Is there enough storage space?
- Does the door interfere with anything?
- Does the shower door open in an easily accessible spot?
- Can the lavatory be conveniently reached from the bedroom?
- How about adding a skylight? If you do, is it double-glazed and ventilated?

- Can space for a dressing room be carved out of the bedroom area?
- Can a second lavatory/vanity area be added?
- Can two at a time use the children's bath?
- Is the laundry room convenient? Or is there a chute?
- Would an extra foot or two make a considerable difference?
- Is the window properly placed for light, ventilation, and privacy? Would clerestory windows improve the space and fit the architecture of the house? What about adding a glass block wall?
- Is the toilet outside of direct visibility from the room?
- Is the basic structure capable of supporting a whirlpool bath for two, or does it need beefing up? Remember, a full whirlpool can weigh up to three tons.
- Is there room for the whirlpool heater and access room to it and the pump? Is the piping specified the proper size?
- Is the necessary special wiring planned?
- If the tub is to be set into a platform, is there sufficient clearance for the steps?
- Will the cabinets fit into the available space after the fixtures are installed? How high should the vanity be raised?

Consider every possible contingency until you are satisfied with your design. The time spent designing the baths will be time saved in selling the home.

Figure 45. Minimal one-wall bath

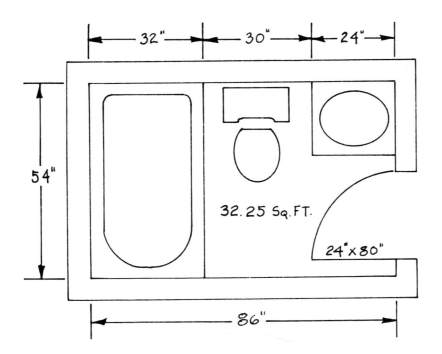

Desirable one-wall bath

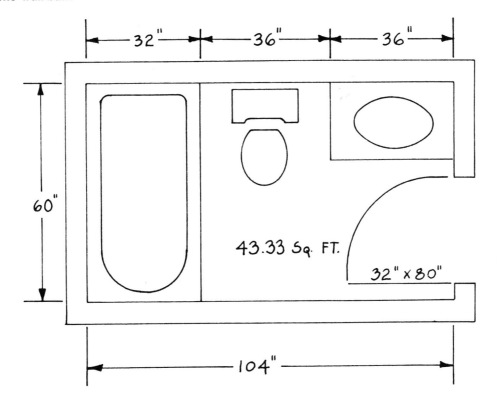

Courtesy National Kitchen and Bath Association

Figure 46. Minimal two-wall bath

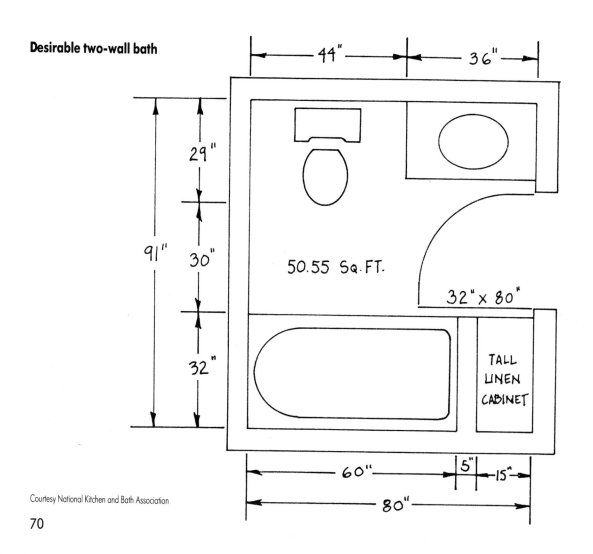

Desirable two-wall bath

Sample Floor Plans

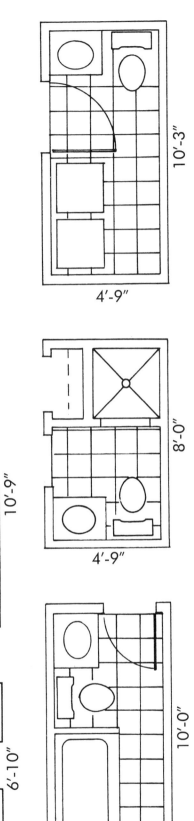

10'-3"

4'-9"

10'-9"

8'-0"

4'-6"

4'-9"

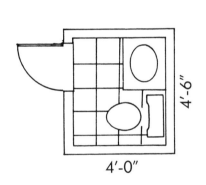

4'-6"

4'-0"

10'-0"

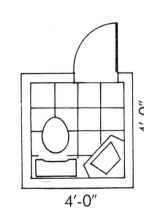

6'-0"

2'-9"

4'-0"

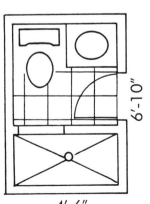

6'-10"

4'-6"

4'-9"

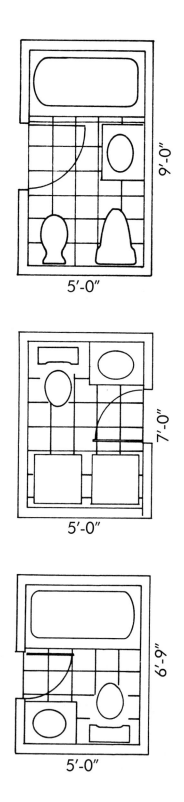

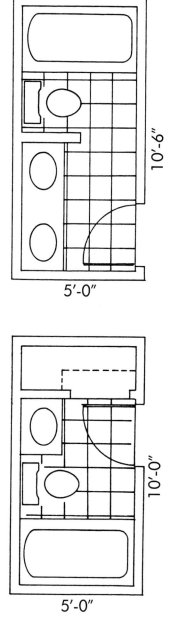

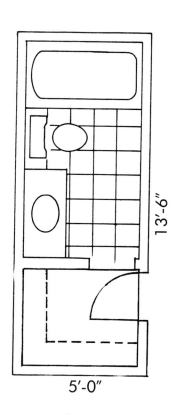

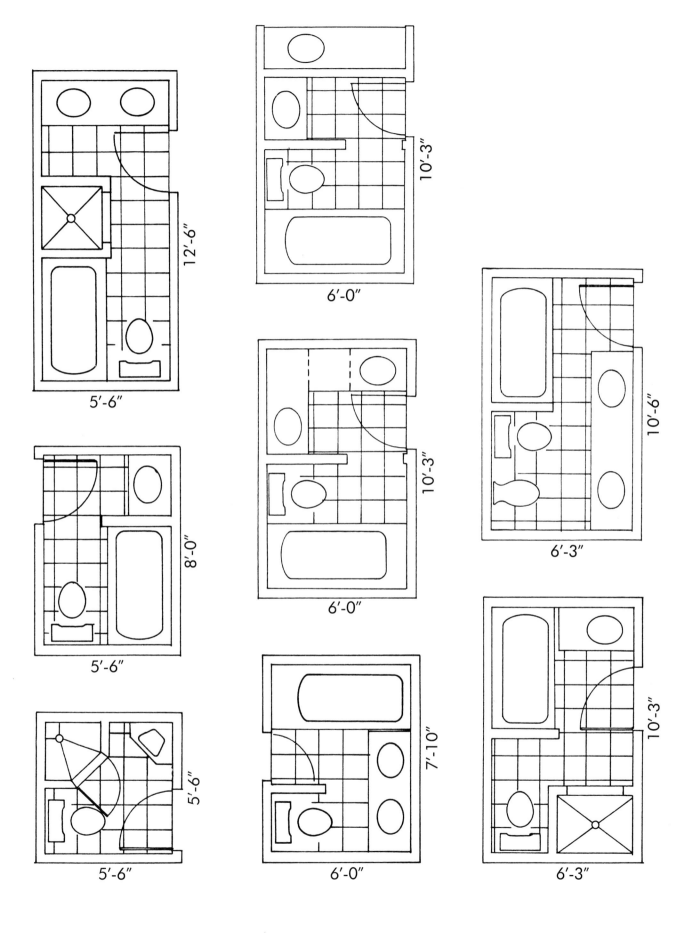

12'-6"

5'-6"

10'-3"

6'-0"

10'-6"

6'-3"

8'-0"

5'-6"

10'-3"

6'-0"

5'-6"

7'-10"

6'-0"

10'-3"

6'-3"

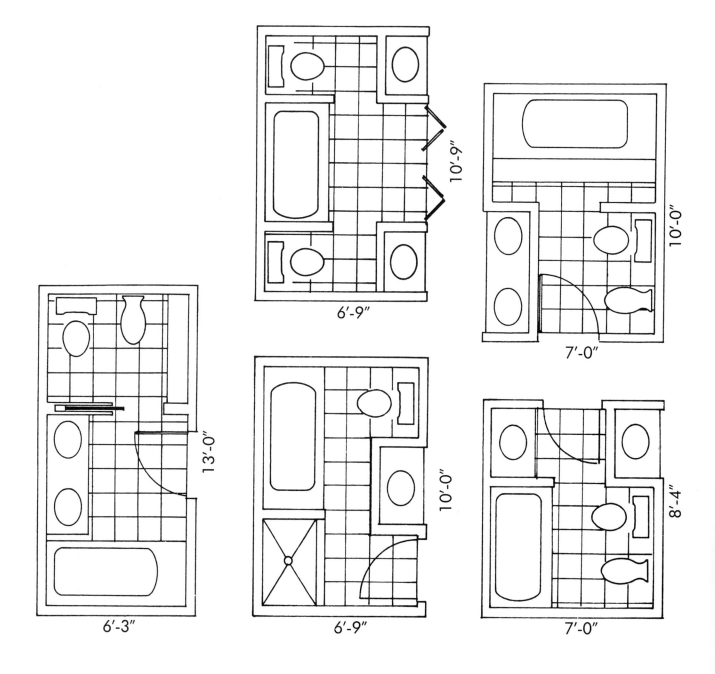

10'-9"

6'-9"

10'-0"

7'-0"

13'-0"

6'-3"

10'-0"

6'-9"

8'-4"

7'-0"

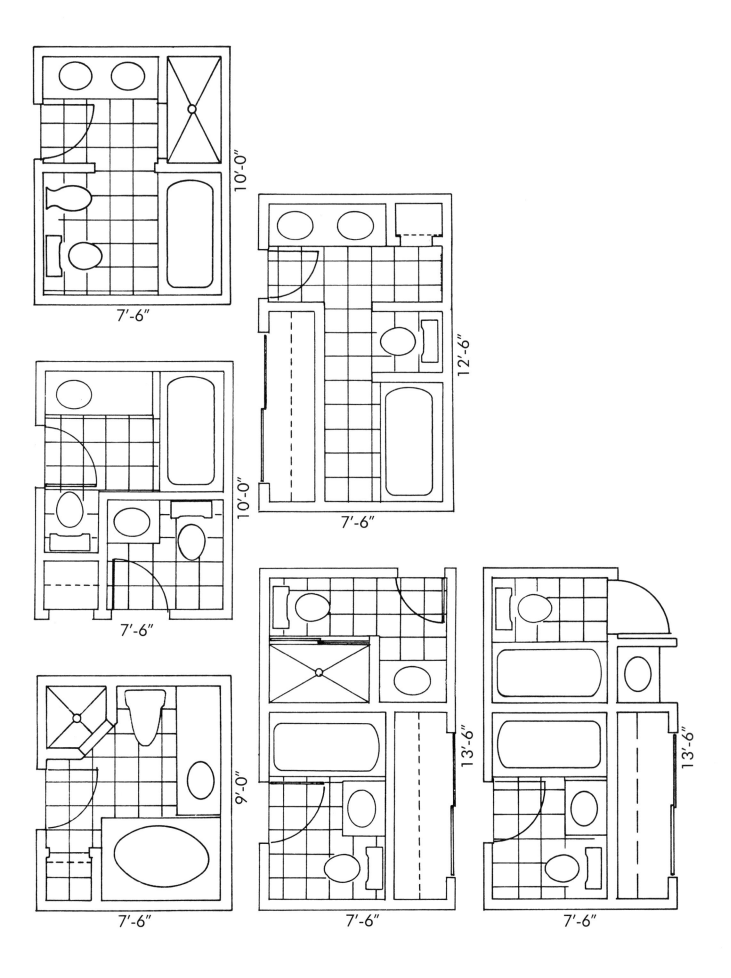

10'-0"

7'-6"

12'-6"

7'-6"

10'-0"

7'-6"

9'-0"

13'-6"

7'-6"

13'-6"

7'-6"

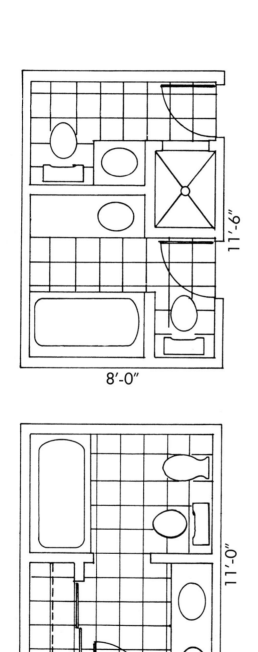

11'-6"

8'-0"

11'-0"

8'-0"

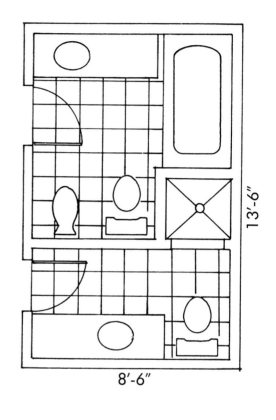

13'-6"

8'-6"

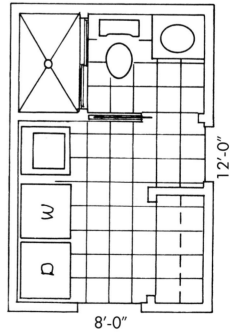

12'-0"

8'-0"

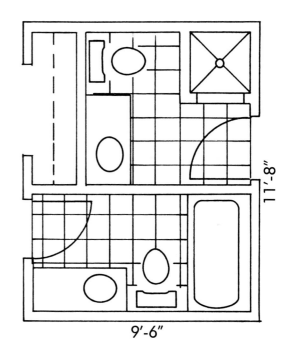

11'-8"

9'-6"

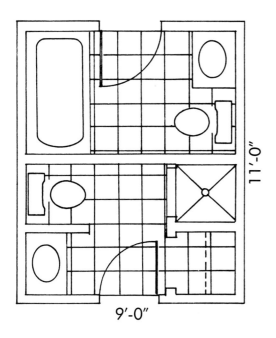

11'-0"

9'-0"

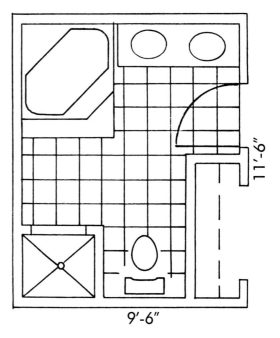

11'-6"

9'-6"

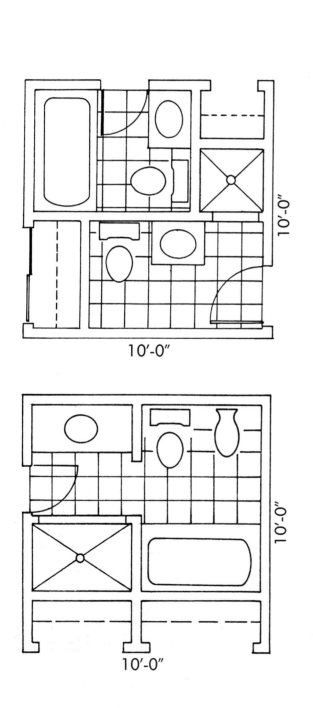

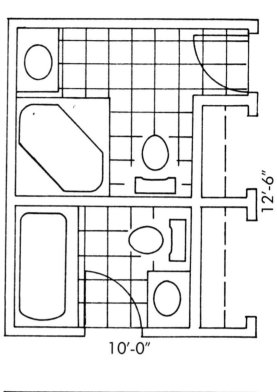

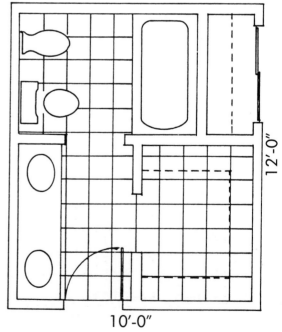

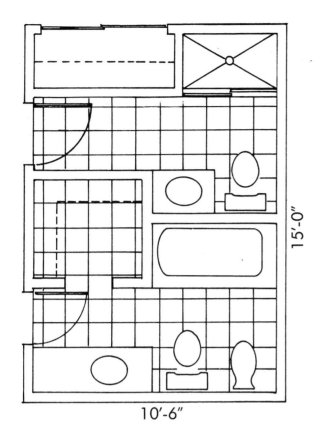

15'-0"

10'-6"

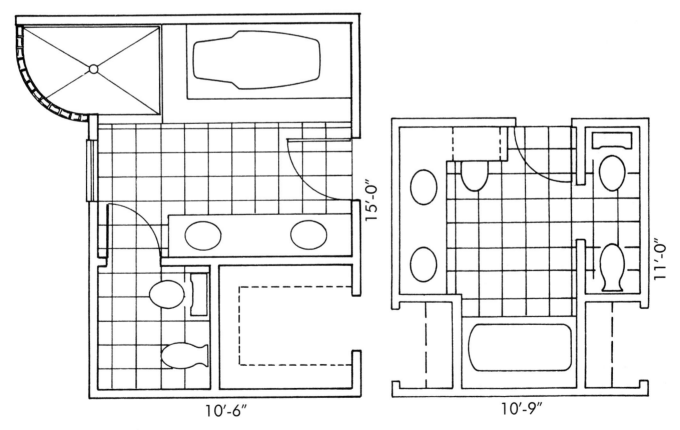

15'-0"

10'-6"

11'-0"

10'-9"

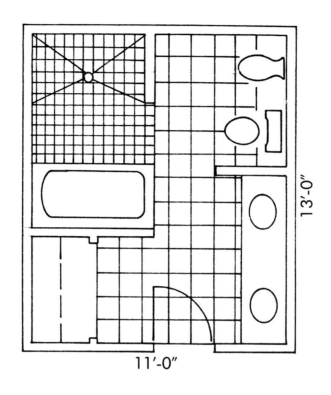

13'-0"

11'-0"

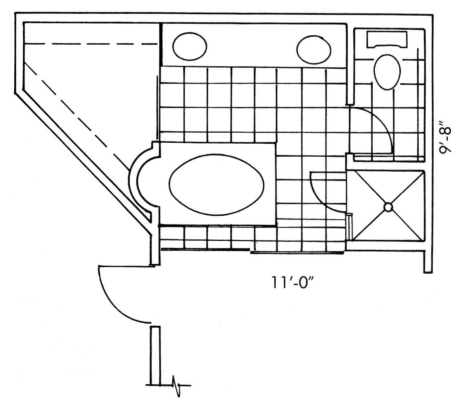

9'-8"

11'-0"

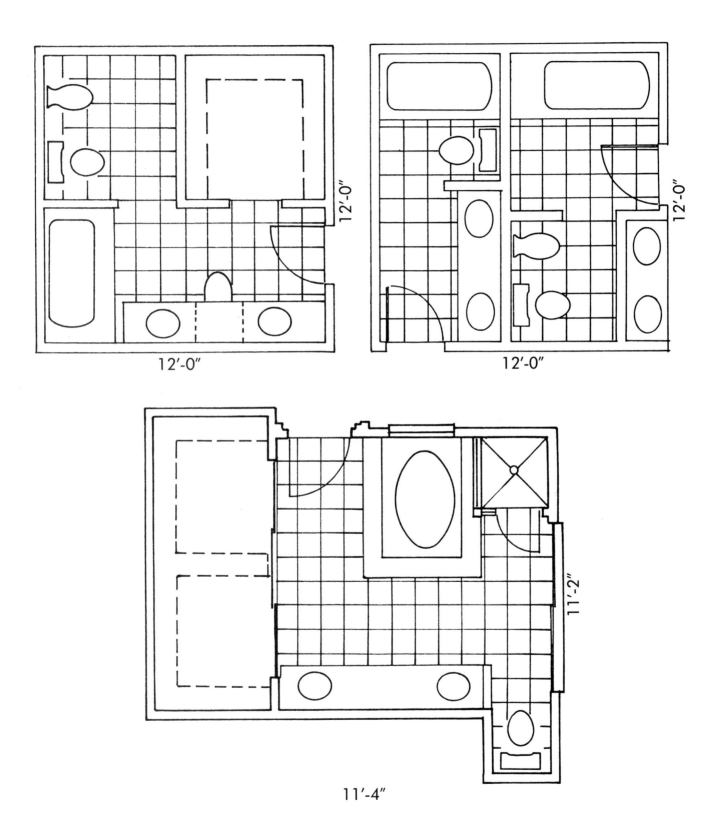

12'-0"

12'-0"

12'-0"

12'-0"

11'-2"

11'-4"

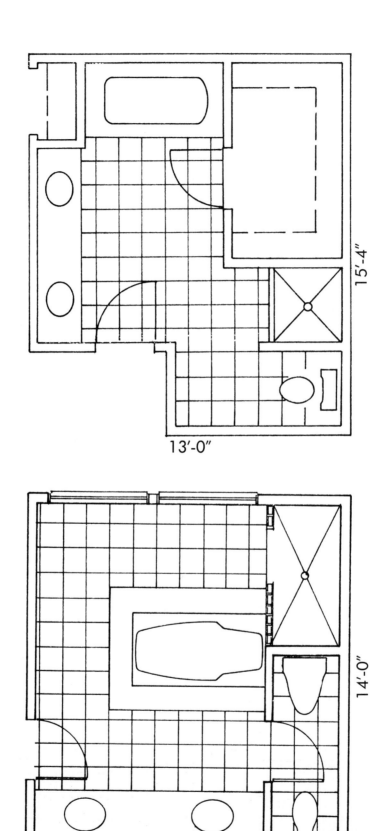

15'-4"

13'-0"

14'-0"

13'-0"

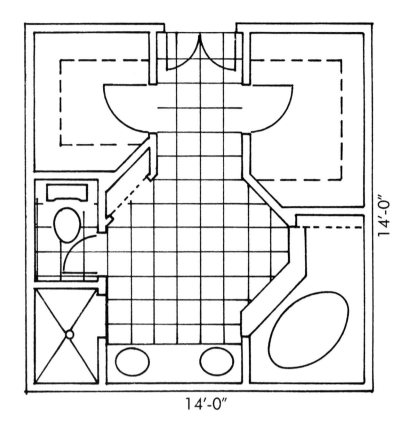

14'-0"

14'-0"

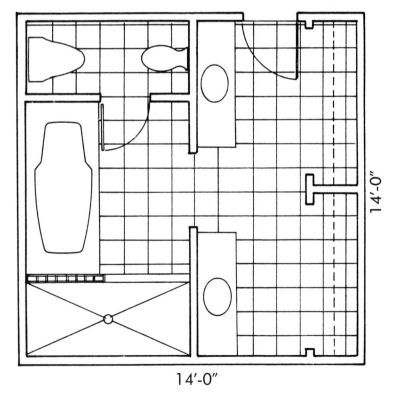

14'-0"

14'-0"

Chapter 9

The Basic Bathroom

The words basic bathroom used to mean a 5-foot × 7-foot room with three fixtures. Although such baths still exist, builders are finding innovative ways to turn them into appealing rooms.

The basic bath is limited by its size and the amount of money available for fixtures, accessories, and finishing. Imaginative uses of space can overcome many shortcomings and offer the customer visual excitement, as well as practicality.

The essentials of good lighting, heating, and ventilation must be the first consideration in planning the basic bath. Safety features such as non-slip tile and grab bars should be included.

With limited space, often there is little choice in placement of fixtures. Stealing a few square feet from the bedroom can improve options for fixture placement, which often makes the difference between a ho-hum bath and one that will sell the home. A 5-foot × 7-foot room doesn't leave many options open; a 5-foot × 10-foot room does.

When there is limited square footage, one room-expanding trick is to extend the room upward. Adding plant shelves, clerestory windows, skylights, or transoms into the adjoining bedroom are all ways to visually enlarge a room and enhance its elegance.

Although glass block is expensive, used in limited amounts it can add light and glamor to a room for a relatively few dollars. When the budget is tight, use it as an inset, rather than for an entire wall.

Many of the spectacular, showy baths today are enormous, upscale rooms. But many others employ illusion and skillful use of space and devices, such as light sources and mirrors, for the desired effect.

The following examples are suggestions for changing ordinary bathrooms with limited square footage into better-looking and often more practical rooms.

Figure 47 shows a 5-foot × 8-foot room with basic fixtures. The architect and designer have opened the room up vertically by lifting the ceiling, adding clerestory windows above the plant shelf, and mirroring the entire vanity wall. The mirror brings in the outdoors, adding to the sense of space. The window seat adds a further touch of luxury.

Figure 48 shows the floor plan of a 6-foot × 10-foot, 3-inch bath with two vanities. By moving one vanity outside the bath, the same space now accommodates two people.

The 6-foot wall space in the bedroom is large enough for the vanity and a wardrobe unit cabinet. Or the space can be used for a linen

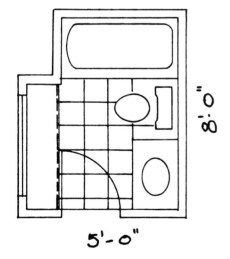

8'-0"

5'-0"

Figure 47. The designer of this bath has opened up the room by extending it vertically and adding skylight and clerestory windows. Note use of tub and shower unit and banjo shelf over toilet.

Courtesy Owens Corning

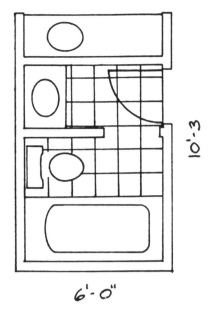

Figure 48. Moving one of the vanities outside the bath provides more convenience, as well as additional counter and storage space. Plumbing is on one wall.

10'-3"

6'-0"

closet. This space can also be completely mirrored above a long vanity, if enough space remains for ample closets. The end walls on each side of the vanity can be used for medicine cabinets or for a shallow cabinet on the vanity side and a deeper cabinet on the other. This bath has its plumbing on one wall, a savings that frees up money for better fixtures.

In Figure 49 a minimal 5-foot × 10-foot area is represented, with a closet squeezed into this small space. Obviously, this bath would not help sell a home.

In the photograph of this same area in Figure 49, the architect and designer have opened up the space. By adding a graceful arch framing the tub area that echoes the curve of the decorative window, the room has been visually expanded and enriched. Note the large tiled ledge behind the tub that serves as a display area. It can also be used for practical purposes: as a place for stacking towels or a basket of bath accessories. The skylight is another plus.

The half wall gives some measure of compartmentation to the room. Extending the tile up the far wall also adds to the sense of space.

Figure 50 illustrates a bath for children. In the first view, this 12-foot, 6-inch × 7-foot, 6-inch room could reasonably be shared by two girls. Its open plan makes it unsuitable for a boy and a girl, or for a member of the family and a guest.

In addition, the vanities are crowded together with storage at one end. The closet opens into the bathtub area, yet there is no dressing space.

By making some minor changes, this room becomes a practical bath serving children of both sexes or guests. First, the vanities are sepa-

Figure 49. An arch frames the tub area, its shape echoing the arch of the window. A wide ledge under the window is practical and attractive. The half-wall provides privacy between the toilet and lavatory.

Courtesy Owens Corning

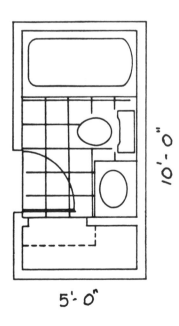

10'-0"

5'-0"

Figure 50. Shifting the closet door to the bedroom, adding a pocket door at the toilet entry, and moving the lavatories to each end of the counter make this a suitable bath for children of either sex or for sharing with a guest.

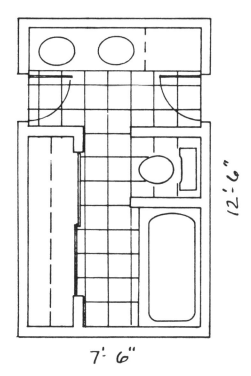

7'-6"

12'-6"

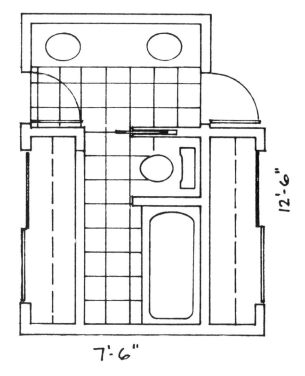

7'-6"

12'-6"

rated, allowing two people to use them simultaneously. The storage space between them is ample for towels. This change makes the entire area seem larger. Adding a pocket door between the vanity and tub area provides the needed privacy.

The closet now opens into one of the bedrooms, where it also acts as a sound barrier. Note that the closet in the other room is also providing a barrier wall.

This same layout could be used for a master bath, by closing in the wall to the second bedroom. By adding 1½ feet to the width of the bath (Figure 51), the room serves as a generous master bath with a compartmentalized water closet and bidet and two small closets framing the lavatory area. The five fixtures do not crowd the space.

Figure 52 illustrates a 10-foot × 10-foot bath. The effect is pure luxury, much of it done with mirrors, glass, and imagination. The basic elements in this room are a 48-inch shower and a 60-inch fiberglass whirlpool. The shower and water closet are separated from the tub and vanities both visually and architecturally with tile and carpet and steps.

The broad transom and French doors between bedroom and bath add to the illusion of space, and the fanlight with the wide, small-paned window contributes both light and a view to the room. If location had prohibited the window, the fanlight could still have been used. Mirroring the wall over the tub further expands the room.

The result of good architectural planning and effective interior design, this room is an elegant treatment of a basic bath, transforming it into the move-up category. Yet this bath was designed for a 1,530-square-foot home selling for under $95,000.

Figure 51. CAD converted this space to a master bath, adding a bidet compartmentalized with a toilet, two convenient closets beside the lavatories, and ample space within the bath. The elevation and perspective drawings show how the finished room will look.

Courtesy American Standard

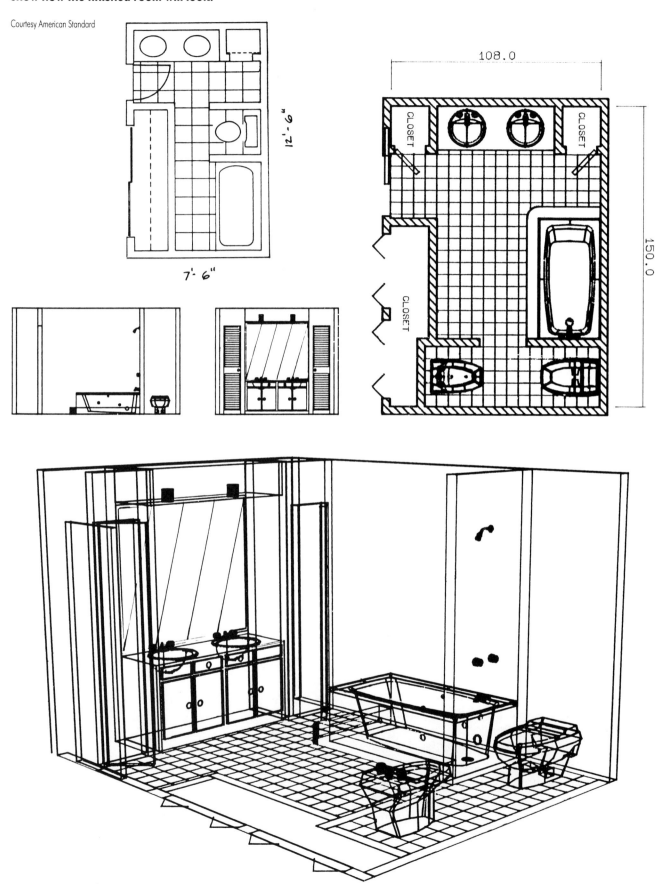

Figure 52. Clever design turns a 10-foot x 10-foot space into an elegant, upscale room with skylights, French doors, and a two-level arrangement that sets the tub off.

Courtesy Owens Corning

The addition of even 1 square foot of space can transform a crowded, ordinary room into one that has sales appeal. The 7-foot, 6-inch × 9-foot room in Figure 53 is usable by one person at a time, crowded with a shower, a separate tub, and a linen closet. In Figure 54 the room has been redesigned adding 1 foot in each direction. Two vanities have been placed outside the bath; a bidet has been added. The room is flooded with light from a skylight and has plenty of room for toweling and partial dressing. Additional storage area was gained in the vanity section. A round window over the tub adds appeal. The closet is shown with a door; it could be designed with open shelving at the top and a door on the lower compartment. The balance between its height and that of the shower would be maintained either way, and the framing of the tub would dramatize the room.

The floor plans shown in this chapter are examples of good fixture placement. The changes in structure, such as lifting the ceiling, adding skylights, putting in pocket doors, creating plant shelves, and adding storage, must also be part of the initial planning.

When these variations are a part of the original plans, their cost is minimized. An architecturally imaginative room inspires the interior design. The results speak for themselves.

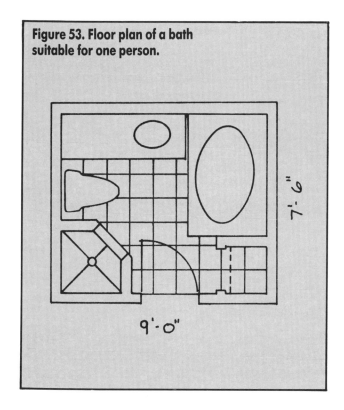

Figure 53. Floor plan of a bath suitable for one person.

7'-6"

9'-0"

Figure 54. This CAD adds 1 foot of space each way to the floor plan in Figure 53. The shower is easily accessible; a bidet has been added; the lavatories are now outside the bath, and the whole room is flooded with light from above. The elevation shows how the walls will look, and the perspective shows the relation of the fixtures.

Courtesy American Standard

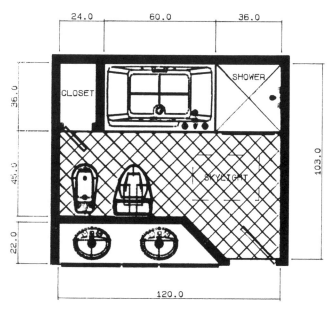

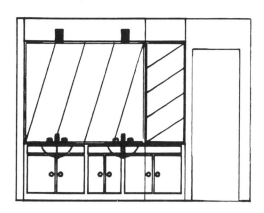

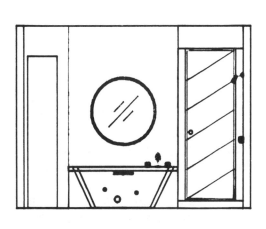

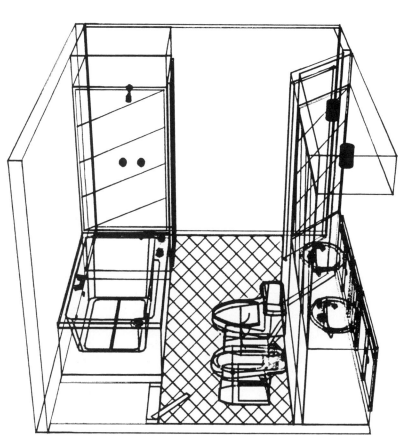

Chapter 10

The Move-up Bathroom

Who Are the Move-up Buyers?

An analysis of today's market clearly shows that the move-up market is multifaceted. The old profile of move-up buyers consisting of a husband, a wife, and 2.5 children in school, with a home in suburbia, is no longer the only move-up market.

The number of households with an annual income of $50,000 or more, headed by persons between the ages of 35 and 44, will have grown from 1.8 million in 1980 to more than 5.4 million in 1990 (National Association of Home Builders 1985). These family units will consist of both higher-income individuals and two-income families. And they will be better informed.

The typical move-up buyer today is a couple between 26 and 45 years old, with incomes between $35,000 and $65,000; most of this group (84 percent) are in two-income households. They have children, live in a home that cost $108,000, and are able to afford one costing $133,000 (*Builder* 1986). They want 17 percent more square footage than they presently have and expect three or four bedrooms and two and a half baths out of this space. The bathroom is now a room for relaxation and pleasure—not merely a "necessary."

The study also looked at young professionals (under 35) and empty nesters (over 55) to determine their specific needs. According to the survey, the younger group wants 22 percent more square footage, while the empty nesters want 3 percent less.

In bedroom suites, both groups want the same things. Preference items are walk-in closets with dressing areas, ceramic tile walls for tub and shower, ceramic tile baths, separate shower enclosures, two lavatories, and a closet in the master bath.

The younger group wants balconies, fireplaces, and whirlpools. The empty nesters opted for upgraded fittings, water-saving fixtures, and a linen closet plus vanity storage (*Builder* 1986).

The study concludes that 22 percent of the move-up market wants a master bedroom on the first floor. Sixty percent of the empty nesters interviewed want it on the first floor.

Another segment of this market is the single head of household. This market tripled from 1960 to 1980 to more than 7.5 million. It represents 4.7 percent of the single-family home market (*Builder* 1986). The Joint Center for Urban Studies predicts a continued, gradual increase in independent households, especially among well-educated singles born during the baby boom of 1945-1964 (*Builder* 1986). In addition, divorced men and women are more and more likely to maintain independent households. Those over 65 and living alone will create another significant portion of the move-up market.

All of these consumers know what is available and what they want. To be competitive, you'll have to offer more than a whirlpool and some pretty tile. Good design is imperative. Quality is essential. Of the respondents to one survey, 96 percent considers quality the most important criterion of those "features that would be somewhat to very important if buying another home" (National Association of Home Builders 1985).

Designing a Move-up Bath

Creating a practical as well as dramatic move-up bath is just as challenging as accomplishing the same objectives in the basic bath. Adding more and costlier fixtures is not the answer. The key is in planning the spatial relationships so that the room works well. Today, that means a master bath for two adults with busy, demanding schedules and a yen for luxury.

One family member should be able to shower, while the other bathes, brushes teeth, or puts on make-up. Closet space should be ample, with adjacent dressing space. Even in a limited space, there should be clearance for easy passage back and forth to the facilities for two people. At the very least, the move-up bath should have a whirlpool, a shower, and two vanities. Two water closets and a bidet are the next step up. The addition of saunas, dressing rooms, built-in storage, exercise areas, fireplaces, and such amenities depends on the market.

In assessing the design for the master move-up bath, use the following checklist of questions. (Many of these features, such as safety grab bars, good ventilation and heating, and functional lighting apply to all bathrooms.)

- Is there privacy for water closets and bidets?
- Does it have free passageway for two persons?
- Could you add a shared relaxation area?
- Is there a convenient dressing room with mirrors?
- Is closet space accessible?
- Is the lighting functional?
- Are the doors opening into "free zones?"
- Have you employed sound-controlling methods?
- Is the bath properly ventilated/heated?
- Is there access to the whirlpool pump?
- Have you included safety grab bars?
- Are there safety faucets with temperature control?

The selling drama comes from special touches, such as skylights, imaginative treatment of compartments, and interesting windows. Baths need not be huge rooms. Small areas can be creatively handled to make them seem larger and more comfortable.

The 10-foot × 10-foot bath illustrated in Chapter 9 (Figure 52) is a case in point. The effect of this design is pure luxury: good architectural planning was enhanced by good interior design. Had the interior designer had to work with a standard floor plan, all of her talent could not have created this feeling of opulence.

Figure 55. This bath is integrated with the bedroom to create a suite, yet the steps separate the rooms, as does the change from carpet to tile. Note compartmentalized toilet and widely spaced lavatories.

Courtesy Owens Corning

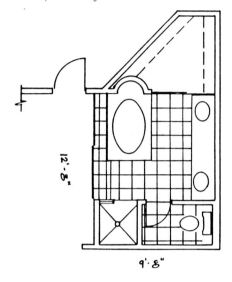

In the example in Figure 55, the master bedroom and bath have been completely integrated. The architect has raised the bath above the bedroom floor level to create a sense of separation, which the designer has heightened by the use of distinctive tiles. The carpeting is used only in the bedroom area.

The greenhouse window floods both rooms with light and adds to the sense of spaciousness. This appealing light makes the plant shelf a natural addition to the room and one that adds richness.

The architect has cleverly created special niches above the tub and leading up to the fanlight, carrying the eye up. The closet acts as a sound barrier wall, although both shower and water closet are enclosed. Despite the open arrangement, this bath gives the users privacy. All this, yet the bath is only 9 feet, 8 inches × 11 feet. In addition, the interior designer has increased the sense of space and elegance by the play of textures and colors.

Imagine the difference if it had been walled off from the bedroom with the tub butted against the wall. Even if a greenhouse window had been included, it would have seemed small. The bedroom would have been nothing but a boxy little room with very little light, instead of part of an inviting suite of rooms.

Note that many consumer preferences are included: tile, separate shower enclosure, two lavatories, private toilet compartment, and a walk-in closet with room for dressing.

The bathroom shown in Figure 56 has mirrors lining both tub walls, doubling the apparent size of the room. The skylight floods the tub with

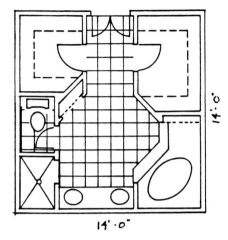

light during the day, and strategically placed spots illuminate it at night. The lavatory area is separated by a half wall, a device that adds even more drama to the platformed tub.

Theatrical lighting is placed above the half wall, ensuring that it will not glare into the user's eyes, and adding light to both bath and lavatory areas.

The floor plan shows how the placement of the huge closets allows for ample dressing area. A separate, enclosed shower is at the opposite end of the vanity from the tub, while the water closet is in its own compartment.

The mirrored walls add to the cost, but they double the aesthetic appeal, which makes the cost negligible.

The floor plan in Figure 57 illustrates a well-functioning bath for a busy couple. By adding 1 foot, however, the room is much improved (Figure 58). The closets can be mirrored bifolds, which enlarge the usable space and the appearance of the room. The lavatory on her side can be off-centered to allow for a dressing table arrangement.

Off-centering the lavatory on his side allows for more storage space to be used for towels and other supplies under the vanity top. Note the tamboured ends, which are attractive, as well as safe. These are repeated on the soffit. Both vanities could have deep medicine chests or open shelves on the end walls.

The shower has been reduced in size and is now combined with a sauna. The water closet and bidet are completely enclosed. By placing the generous 72-inch whirlpool on the outer wall, a bay window is now a part of the room's appeal.

The door into the dressing area has been made into a pocket door.

These three bathrooms illustrate the importance of architectural and interior design planning. The decisions to eliminate walls, install skylights and distinctive windows, use decorative beams, recess tubs on platforms, create compartments, and dramatize with lighting had to be made on the original plans.

Figure 57. Bathroom floor plan suitable for a busy couple

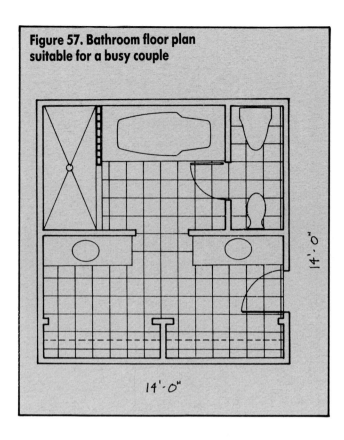

14'-0"

14'-0"

Figure 58. Improvements through CAD include the addition of tambour, rounded corners on lavatory counters, and mirrored bifold doors that enhance a dressing area's practicality. Rearrangement allows a larger tub and spacious shower. This is an ideal bath for use by two people at once.

Courtesy American Standard

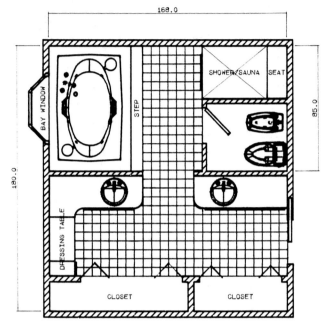

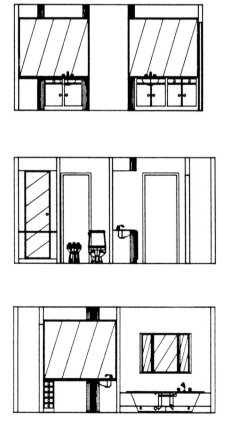

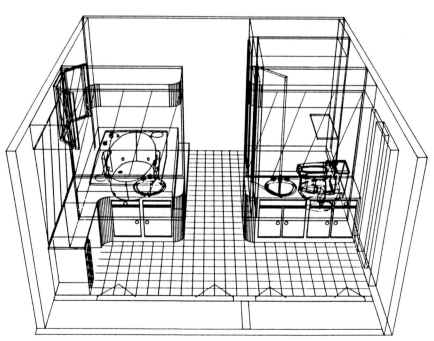

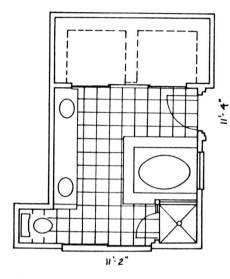

The example in Figure 59 is an 11-foot, 4-inch × 11-foot, 2-inch room that the designer has enlarged visually by adding a wall of mirrored closets, which catch and reflect the light from the ample window over the square tub. The tub is emphasized by its stepped position and by the useful and decorative ledge framing it.

The glassed-in shower is tucked into the corner of the room facing the water closet compartment, which is in a private niche. The two lavatories are widely separated to allow for a bench between them. The closets concealed behind the glass doors along a wall are two 6-foot walk-ins, 2 feet, 6 inches deep.

A spectacular example of an upscale bath, the all-white room in Figure 60 uses solid plastic resembling the floor tile for the wall and tub surrounds. The designer has deliberately used grout lines in the plastic to achieve this effect. Only a completely color-through plastic could have created the design of the round tub.

Again, mirrors have been used to produce illusion. The tub area is only 4 feet × 4 feet. By mirroring both walls at an angle, it looks big and inviting. The eye is led through the room to the window and on into space.

Note the half-moon mirrors facing each other from the make-up bar and the lavatory side. The make-up bar is a practical 11 inches deep, rather than the usual 24 inches. This is the actual width most desirable for applying make-up at a wall mirror. A bar of 24 inches requires the use of a secondary mirror.

The white faucet extends upward and swivels, making it as practical as it is handsome. The entire effect is a subtle marriage of contemporary materials and design with classicism, enhanced by the use of track lights and lamps concealed in the columns.

Figure 61 features a free-standing whirlpool platformed in the center of a 14-foot × 13-foot room. Redesigned, with minor changes (Figure 62), the door becomes a double French door opening in the center of the room. A skylight has been added directly over the tub to highlight it. Closets now open with mirrored bifold doors into the room, reflecting the mirrored vanity wall. Note the vanity walls over the dressing table

area. This bath functions for two and serves as a dressing room, as well as a relaxation room.

The 15-foot, 3-inch × 13 foot bath in Figure 63 is an attractive design. A more dramatic treatment, however, is to rearrange the fixtures and closet, putting the tub and shower together and adding a bidet (Figure 64). Angling the tub on a platform creates a focal point that pulls the eye into the room. The skylight bathes the entire room with light. Ample room to dress in the center of the room is now available, without having to dodge the angle formerly created by the closet. The space is no longer chopped up but smoothly flowing. The shower is now a generous 4½ feet long.

The creators of these baths used devices that added a sense of space, luxury, and elegance. Skylights, plant shelves, innovative window treatments, platformed tubs, mirrors, and tile and solid plastics, combined with imagination solidify the look of these bathrooms. Each has ideas that can be borrowed to enhance the designs of other baths.

Consider adding a sauna, a steam room, or other upscale amenities to increase the bath's usefulness and appeal. But whatever fixtures it offers, make sure the bath incorporates practicality with beauty and comfort.

Think of the bath not as a single, isolated room but as an adjunct, an extension of the bedroom. Think in terms of suites. Then moving walls, creating flowing upward and outward spaces, opening up the bathing area and closing off the water closet, using glass and mirrors—all become part of the planning stage.

Figure 60. This dramatic all-white bath has laminate on the walls and tub surrounds to match the floor tile. Angled mirrors beside the tub expand the room. Note the 11-inch-wide make-up bar.

Courtesy Formica 2000®

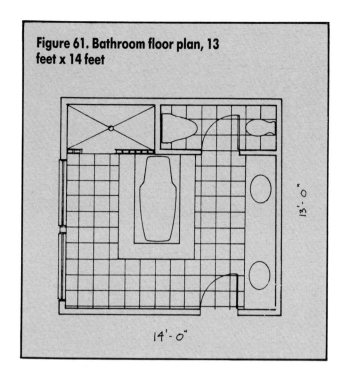

Figure 61. Bathroom floor plan, 13 feet x 14 feet

13'-0"

14'-0"

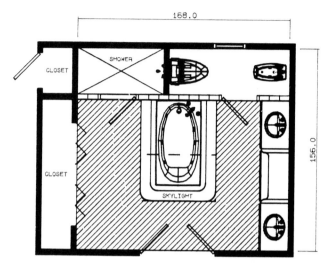

Figure 62. Improved through CAD, French doors border the tub, which is dramatized by a skylight directly above. These effects turn an adequate bath into one with sales appeal. The lavatory layout provides a make-up bar.

Courtesy American Standard

168.0

156.0

CLOSET

SHOWER

CLOSET

SKYLIGHT

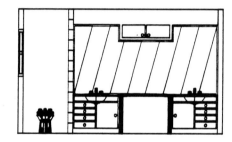

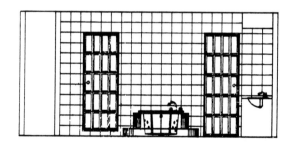

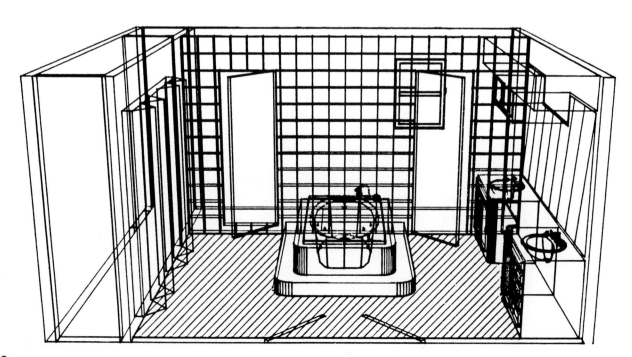

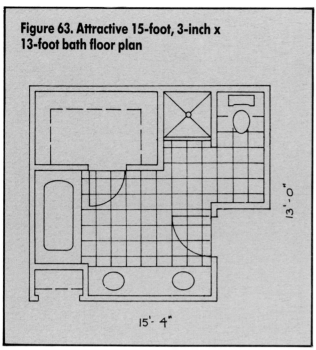

Figure 63. Attractive 15-foot, 3-inch x 13-foot bath floor plan

13'-0"

15'-4"

Figure 64. Rearranging the fixtures through CAD has eliminated the slightly awkward angles, creating an inviting room. The closet is now easily accessible, and the ample ledges around the tub provide storage.

Courtesy American Standard

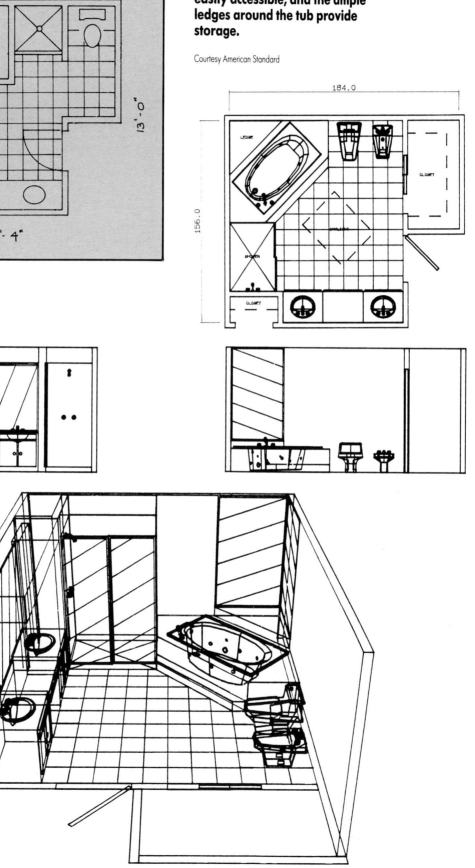

Chapter 11

Designing for the Elderly and Handicapped

The Market

Many terms are applied to the older population, such as seniors, mature, and elderly; but this market, from age 55 up, is a diverse one. Who comprises this market, and what should you consider in designing baths for them?

One expert suggests that the mature market diverges into four different segments (Lazer 1985). The 55- to 64-year-olds, about 22 million strong, are the pre-retirees, the segment that commands the highest median income ($24,094), has the greatest disposable income, and is actively seeking ways to enjoy life (U.S. Bureau of the Census 1983). This group is a target market for homes with move-up bathrooms, with a projected growth of 25 percent by 1995 (Lazer 1985). (See Chapter 10 for consumer preferences in move-up baths.)

The next group, those 65-74 years old, are designated the elderly. In 1985 they numbered 17 million. By 1995 their ranks will have grown 10 percent, to 19 million (Lazer 1985). This group is still active but may be slowing down. This is the prime market for retirement developments and condominium living, where maintenance is someone else's problem, and for homes that are convenient for current needs and adaptable, if necessary. Seven out of ten people over 65 own their own homes, and 85 percent of them have paid off their mortgages. Although their median incomes have dropped 50 percent from that of the 55- to 64-year-olds, they benefit from various programs, such as discounts for transportation and prescriptions and Medicare. The demands on their disposable incomes are less. In addition, they can cash in the equity in their present homes for new homes. This is a market that offers excellent potential.

The third segment, ranging from ages 75 to 84, are known as the aged; this is another high-growth group. In 1985 they numbered 9 million. By 1995 their numbers will have increased 25 percent, to 11 million (Lazer 1985). This market is a target for more communal living, where health care is readily available on site, and various services, such as transportation and meals, are available in the facility.

The very old group of the population, aged 85 and over, is the most rapidly growing. By 1995 about 4 million people will be in this segment, a growth of 50 percent during the decade (Lazer 1985). This is a specialized housing market that consists of those who continue to live in housing they already own or who are able to live in a retirement community or who will enter institutions. Of this group 23 percent is institutionalized, as opposed to 7 percent of the 75- to 84-year-olds (American Association of Retired Persons 1985). Designing for this segment of the market consists of adapting current facilities or institutional design and is beyond the scope of this book.

In all of the above-mentioned categories are handicapped or persons with limitations living at home. For instance, almost 13 million people suffer from arthritis in the United States (National Center for Health Statistics 1984).

Over 50 percent of the U.S. population is in this enormous and rapidly growing group. John Zeisel, president of Building Diagnostics, Inc., warns against lumping all members of the mature market into one pot. He outlines three rules for builders targeting the older market:

- Build for the diversity of the market.
- Build in independence.
- Focus on residential imagery, not institutional.

Keep these rules in mind. In designing bathrooms, the second rule is especially important: build in independence.

This chapter deals with the design of bathrooms for the market aged 65 and up, for people who may have physical limitations or some handicap.

General Design Requirements

With forethought, the bathroom can be planned to be useful for the healthy, for those with limited ability, and for the wheelchair occupant. Buildings specifically for the handicapped demand specific planning. Building for the elderly, however, can be planned for the healthy with consideration for use by the temporarily handicapped. Designs for the elderly should recognize future needs, as well as provide safety features for the present. Two elements of bathroom design for this market predominate: access and safety.

Access

While most of the elderly can function quite well in a standard home, even a generally healthy person may occasionally need a wheelchair, such as after an operation. Or they may find themselves in one for a longer period. Under these circumstances, access is vital.

ANSI has established specifications for design for the physically handicapped. These are the best guides available and should be followed in building for the elderly. Following these allows for present safety needs and prepares for future needs. The ANSI requirements that make a bath (and home) practical for this group are few. Builders can readily meet these without drastic changes in building design.

Doorways must be a minimum of 32 inches wide, with the door opened to 90 degrees, measured between the face of the door and the stop (Figure 65). A preferable width is 36 inches. The hardware used on doors should be easy to operate. ANSI suggests lever, push-type, or U-shaped handles.

The doorway threshold should not be more than ½ inch high for entry into the bathroom (and for all interior doors). Raised thresholds and floor-level changes between ¼ inch and ½ inch should be beveled, with a slope that is no more than 1:2.

Figure 65. Doorway clearance

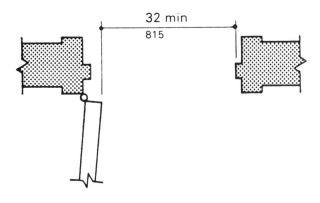

Figure 67. Toilet paper dispenser height

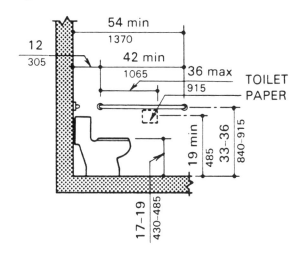

Figure 66. Space needed for a smooth U-turn in a wheelchair

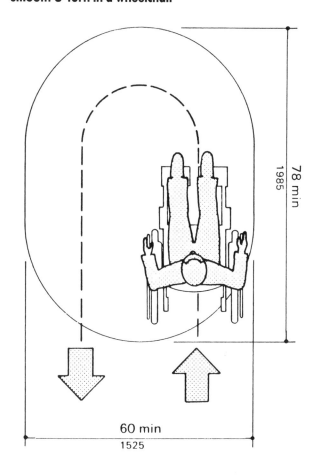

Make sure the bath area is large enough for a wheelchair to turn in: a minimal clear floor space of 60 inches in diameter is needed. An area 78 inches × 60 inches is preferable. (See Figure 66.)

The height of the water closet should be 17 to 19 inches, measured from the top of the toilet seat. Most modern toilets will be shorter. Lower toilets are readily adaptable by the addition of a special seat, which the owners can add if needed. (If the home is being built for the handicapped, then special water closets should be installed.) The location of toilet tissue holders is important. The recommended distance is shown in Figure 67. Too often toilet tissue is inconveniently placed, and these specifications apply for designs for all markets.

Required clearance for using the water closet is 48 inches from the front of the fixture to the opposite wall. The toilet should have 18 inches of clearance from the wall.

A wheelchair occupant needs a lavatory just 27 inches from the floor, with the mirror above it, 40 inches from the floor. Since the most desirable height for a standard sink is 34 to 36 inches, an adjustment must be made. Since a wheelchair occupant also needs clearance space under the lavatory, it is impossible to build a good-looking bathroom that suits the healthy and the handicapped. Even the pedestal lavatory does not suffice, because it is usually 32 inches high. Installing a lavatory in a vanity makes for a more adaptable unit because the vanity can be removed and the lavatory lowered if desired.

The clear floor space for use of a tub is 30 inches by 60 inches (Figure 68).

Showers should be at least 36 inches × 36 inches, with a seat 17 to 19 inches from the floor. This is 2 to 4 inches higher than the usual seat but is certainly usable by anyone.

The shower receptor height can be a problem. It should not be more than the normal 4 inches high for the wheelchair occupant. The wheelchair patient can then slide from the chair into the seat of the smaller shower enclosure. But in larger showers, a barrier shouldn't exist, so the wheelchair can wheel in. For wheelchair usage, shower dimensions must be 64 inches by 64 inches. One soap dish in the shower should be placed at 54 inches, with another at 26 inches above the floor for use when seated.

Doors must not swing into the free space for any of the fixtures.

Controls, such as switches, should not be higher than 54 inches from the floor. Receptacles for electric plugs should be at least 15 inches above the floor. These measurements are those that a wheelchair occupant can handle. They are also comfortable for the average person.

Storage is a problem, especially for the wheelchair occupant. A wall cabinet is obviously unusable. Drawers or open shelves within the seated reach of an adult is the best answer. The reaches of the average adult from a wheelchair are as follows: 54 inches (high reach); 24 inches (high reach over obstruction); 9 inches (low reach). (See Figure 69.)

Hanging rods should be 48 to 54 inches above the floor for a wheelchair occupant to use. Towel bars should be 29 to 32 inches high, although the 36-inch height is usable (Figure 70).

Figure 68. Clear floor space for use of tub

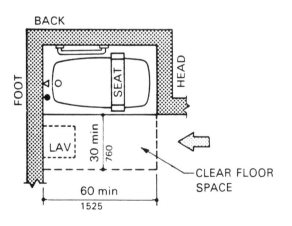

Figure 69. Heights of storage shelves and closets

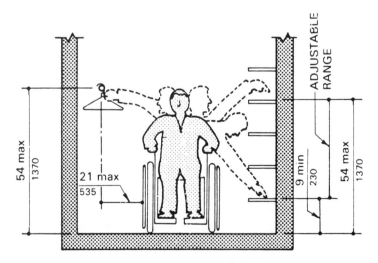

Safety

Safety in the bathroom for this market means installing grab bars, shower seats, slip-resistant flooring, and nightlights.

Grab bars are a must for this market. If bars are not installed when the home is built, provision for them should be built into the structure. The problem with this is obvious: when ownership of the house changes, new owners may not be apprised of the position of the reinforcing. For the little extra cost, bars can be tastefully incorporated in the initial building.

Grab bars and faucet controls for a shower should be located as indicated in Figure 71; a versatile shower unit that can be used in a fixed position or hand held should be included. Choose faucet controls that are easy for the elderly to operate (Figure 71).

Tubs and showers should have a minimal 9-inch horizontal bar in the center of the wall with the faucets or a 9-inch vertical bar at the place of entry into the tub or shower.

Figure 70. Grab bar location in a shower

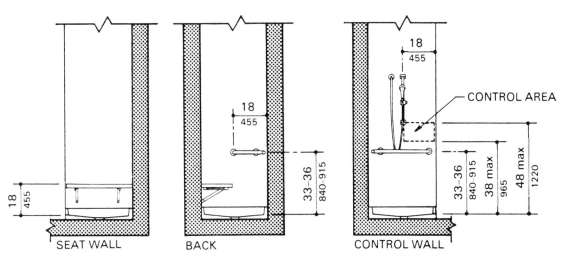

This material is reproduced with permission from *American National Standard for Buildings and Facilities—Providing Accessibility and Usability for Physically Handicapped People*, copyright 1986, by the American National Standards Institute, Inc. at 1430 Broadway, New York, NY 10018

Another grab bar should be installed along the side of a tub. It should be at least 24 inches long and placed a maximum of 24 inches from the front wall. This permits room for a seat in the tub (Figure 72). If the seat is placed at the head of the tub, the bars should be 48 inches long and placed no more than 15 inches from the wall.

All grab bars must be ¾ to 1½ inch in diameter and have 1½ inches between the wall and the bar. The wall they are mounted on should be smooth, to avoid bruising of the knuckles.

Grab bars must be able to support a minimum of 250 pounds. They must be attached to a firm backing: 2-inch × 4-inch blocks nailed between studs or ¾-inch exterior plywood anchored to the stud.

When installing grab bars in the shower, place them 36 inches from the floor. They should also be 33 to 36 inches above the bottom of the tub. Thus, a grab bar built into the side of a 16-inch-deep tub is insufficient to provide the necessary leverage, and an additional bar should be added. Tubs placed against one wall or centered in a room obviously can't provide the bars needed, so avoid these when building for this market.

105

Figure 71. Lever handles are easier for the elderly to operate.

Courtesy Kohler

The design of tubs with broad lips and/or ample platforms enables the user to enter and exit by sitting on the edge and swinging around. But this property poses a hazard: the user cannot grab the edge for assistance and support. This makes grab bars even more essential. The user must have something to help pull the body up to the rim. A bar on each side of the tub is preferable.

A bar is useful only if the user has to extend his hand 12 inches or less to reach it. If he has to reach beyond that, the bar becomes a hazard.

Bars should be placed in logical, obvious spots so that using them is a natural action or reaction (Kira 1967). There should be no possibility of mistaking the faucets for the safety bar.

Install a grab bar in front of the bidet. Since the fixture is used facing the wall, there is no support for raising and lowering the body, except for grabbing onto other fixtures or a counter. Any of these substitutes poses a danger.

Ideally, the water closet should have a grab bar beside it. The same type used for the bidet can be incorporated into a wall by the water closet.

The overall design of the bathroom intended for the elderly market should have the water closet by a wall so a bar can be installed.

Fortunately, manufacturers have become aware of the need for seats in showers, and many plastic shower stalls incorporate seats in them. When building for the elderly market, a seat in the shower is essential. The seat should be on the wall facing the fixtures and extend the entire width of the wall. The shower spray (used as a fixed unit or hand held) should have a 60-inch extension.

Floor materials used in bathrooms should be safe for any use, that is, slip resistant. If carpeting is used, it must be securely attached and have a firm pad or none at all. The pile should be level with a maximum height of ½ inch.

Figure 72. Grab bar location in a tub

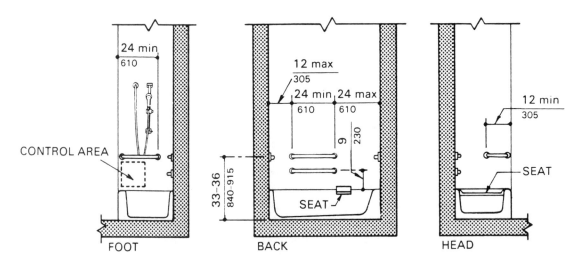

This material is reproduced with permission from *American National Standard for Buildings and Facilities—Providing Accessibility and Usability for Physically Handicapped People*, copyright 1986, by the American National Standards Institute, Inc. at 1430 Broadway, New York, NY 10018

Appendix 1

Plumbing System Materials

The materials for supply pipe must meet stringent local codes, as well as the requirements of the U.S. Food and Drug Administration for safety from leaching of contaminating chemicals into the water. Steel, copper tubing, and plastic are commonly used materials. Each has its advantages. The following, from the *College of Product Knowledge*, discusses these materials.

Steel pipe replaced wrought iron piping for supply lines about 100 years ago but is now used infrequently in housing. It has proved its strength; it is not easily crushed and resists shocks and stress. Its ability to handle pressure is extremely high; it has excellent dimensional stability at high temperatures; its connective system is strong; it can be welded and insulated against the sound of flowing water; it's low cost, long lasting, and durable under normal circumstances (Arnold 1979).

Copper tubing predominates today. It normally resists corrosion and is lightweight. It is compact, versatile in joinery and comes in straight lengths and coils. Its ease in installation makes it popular in residential construction (Arnold 1979).

Plastic piping is increasingly popular, although some codes still forbid its use. It is less expensive than any other material, easy to install, lightweight, self-insulating, and usually comes in coils. It also resists corrosion and chemical attack (Arnold 1979).

Piping's resistance to corrosion and to scaling from accumulated minerals and the ability to handle various water temperatures are important. Polyethylene plastic piping is suitable only for cold water supply; polybutylene is suitable for both hot and cold water (Arnold 1979).

DWV piping is generally made of cast iron, copper, or plastic. Cast iron has been the traditional material, but it is now used primarily in commercial construction and heavily unionized areas.

Plastic is most commonly used because it is lighter and easier to handle than cast iron or other metal piping. An installation that weighs 100 pounds in cast iron weighs just 1 pound in a similar plastic assembly. Plastic is also relatively cheap, is labor saving, and offers a lower coefficient of friction (Arnold 1979).

The drain system is the piping that carries toilet waste, as well as all other waste water. It centers on the main stack or "vertical drainage channel." It connects to the building drain, which then feeds into the sewer or septic system.

The main stack is usually 3 inches in diameter and is fed by the smaller 1½- or 2-inch waste pipes from the kitchen sink, lavatories, showers, tubs, and washing machines. Toilet waste pipes require a minimum diameter of 3 inches. Cleanouts for toilet waste lines should be accessible.

Appendix 2

Fixture Materials

Several materials are used in making bathroom fixtures, and a clear understanding of the various fixtures requires knowledge of these.

Vitreous china is primarily used for lavatories, water closets, and bidets. Hard-surfaced, smoothly glazed, high-quality vitreous china should be free of surface defects. It resists chipping and cracking and is easy to clean.

Vitreous china is made by pouring a liquified clay mixture into plaster of Paris molds, where it is cured. It is then removed from the mold, cleaned, dried, and sprayed with a glazing mixture similar to the liquified clay. If color is desired, it is added at this stage. The fixture is then fired in a tunnel kiln at up to 2,250 degrees F and slowly cooled over a period of 24 hours. This transforms it into a smooth, glassy finished product that is strong, solid, and nonporous (Arnold 1979).

Enameled cast iron, used primarily for tubs, is molded cast iron with a porcelain enamel glaze applied, which creates a thick, chip-resistant surface. Since cast iron is a good heat conductor, it keeps water warm longer than other materials do (Arnold 1979). These tubs weigh from 200 to 500 pounds.

Enameled cast iron is made by pouring molten metal in a sand mold in a process known as sand casting. It is then dry blasted into a smooth, uniform surface. A clay mixture similar to that used for vitreous china is then applied in powder form; the fixture is fired to melt the finish into a smooth, glass-like coating. Color is added in the final process.

Enameled steel is similar to cast iron in appearance, but tubs of this material are less expensive and desirable than cast iron ones because the porcelain is thinner and more subject to chipping. The tubs lack the heat-retention properties of cast iron and should be undercoated with a sound-deadening material (Arnold 1979). This type of tub weighs about 100 pounds.

Steel tubs are formed by stamping, then finishing through a process similar to that used for cast iron tubs. The finish is sprayed on, rather than applied in powder form. Better quality products are then ground, polished, and buffed to give the smooth surface desired.

Fiberglass and reinforced plastic, a complicated category of materials, refer to various methods of manufacturing or the fixture coating. Thus, one manufacturer may term a product fiberglass, which actually applies to the reinforcement; another may call a fixture acrylic, which applies to the coating. Still another may dub a fixture vacuum formed, which applies to the manufacturing process (Arnold 1979). The *College of Product Knowledge* attributes some of the confusion to the fact that most people lump all plastics under one heading, probably because they don't understand the specific resins and processes used.

Fiberglass reinforced plastic was one of the first alternatives developed for plumbing use and continues to be widely used today. It is not, however, the only reinforcing material used.

The traditional fiberglass process uses a highly polished mold, which is waxed, then sprayed with a polyester gel coat. This cures and leaves a smooth, hard exterior surface. The molds are then sprayed with a mixture of polyester resin and fiberglass strands that become a reinforcing back for the gel coat layer. Reinforcing strips and braces are placed on the back while it is still wet; once cured, they adhere securely.

The curing is done under controlled general atmospheric conditions. The fixture is then trimmed and any accessories are added. This process is called "spray-up." Another process that produces a similar product is known as "lay-up," and another is done with matched dies, producing a fixture with integrated reinforcing ribs.

The fixtures called acrylic or vacuum-formed acrylic are structurally similar to the traditional fiberglass approach, but the process is different and an acrylic sheet is used for the surface, instead of a polyester gel coat. The acrylic forms a skin.

It is placed in a mold and heated until it becomes somewhat soft and pliable; then it is sucked into the female portion of the mold until it assumes the desired form. It is cooled, then sprayed with resin and chopped fiberglass in much the same way as is traditional fiberglass. Reinforcing boards and braces, trimming, and accessories are added in a similar manner (Arnold 1979).

Wall panels for showers and tubs are also vacuum formed but not sprayed with reinforcing materials. Both acrylic and ABS (multipolymer) resins are used for this.

Injection molding is the most advanced of the processes used in producing plastic plumbing fixtures. Unfortunately, the molds increase in cost with size, so production has been limited to lavatories and toilet tanks. This provides a high-gloss finish with structural strength that is homogeneous in color. This process is accomplished by forcing melted, compressed plastic resin into a mold. After cooling, the fixture is released from the mold and trimmed.

Plastics form the newest, lightest, and most leakproof fixtures. Their use for tubs, showers, and shower receptors has afforded greater ease in installation and easier maintenance for the home owner. These fixtures look like porcelain enamels or vitreous china but do not chip or break. Since they are molded in one piece, there is no grouting to repair or to collect mildew. Most are resistant to household cleansers. Generally, the thicker the surface, the sturdier the unit. Well-insulated shells for tubs prevent heat loss. Check the thickness around the edges for uniformity to determine whether the form was properly molded. Check the surface for scratches, pockmarks, and other blemishes upon delivery. The several types of plastics used for bathroom fixtures are described in the following paragraphs.

Acrylic maintains its gloss and color indefinitely, is easy to maintain, is not susceptible to scratching, and can be repaired. Repairs to marble-like surfaces are easier to camouflage than those to solid-color surfaces because of the color variation of marble patterns.

Gel coat is slightly less expensive than acrylic and more prone to fade from ultraviolet and infrared rays, as well as from chemicals. It requires more maintenance than acrylic, has a duller look, and needs resurfacing about every five years. It is easily repaired.

Cultured marble and onyx, used primarily for countertops and lavatories, are polyester resins filled with various inorganic materials, such as crushed marble. Lighter and less expensive than natural stones, they are available in various qualities, depending on the thickness and evenness of the outer gel coat and its curing. Cultured onyx is more expensive than marble because of its deeper color and its translucence.

Cast acrylic is a filled acrylic monomer. It is a solid, nonporous material composed of natural minerals and high-performance acrylics. It consists of a solid, water-resistant, homogeneous sheet that resists heat, stains, and impact damage. It has the added advantage of being workable with woodworking tools and can be shaped, joined, and sanded on site.

Exotic materials, such as marble, onyx, specially constructed stone, polyethylene-coated teak or oak, and tile are used for tubs in luxury baths. Marble, tile, brass, silver, gold plate, and wood are also used for lavatories. These materials are reserved for top-of-the-line custom homes, as a rule.

Appendix 3

Detailed Information on Lighting, Ventilation, and Insulation

Lighting the Bathroom

Light is measured in lumens, which is the rate at which a 1-candela light falls on a 1-square-foot area that is 12 inches from the light source. The efficiency of a light bulb (or lamp as it is properly called) is measured by lumens per watt. This is figured by dividing lumen output by the wattage. A comparison of the efficiency of incandescent and fluorescent light is as follows:

	Lumens	Efficiency
Incandescent 60 watts, A-19	870	14.50 l/w
Fluorescent 60 watts T-12 48 CWX	4,300	71.67 l/w

The following description from Wood-Mode Cabinetry is one of the best guides to fluorescent lighting (O'Connor 1986).

Deluxe warm white	Simulates incandescent, reinforces warm colors, food, and skin tones.
Deluxe cool white	Simulates natural daylight; keeps colors true; cools down the overall look.
Warm white	Blends fairly well with incandescents; tones down colors.
Cool white	Blends with natural daylight; compromises between the warm and cool whites; dulls reds.
Daylight white	Used commercially. Dulls warm colors, makes flesh tones look grey.
Full-spectrum	Also called color-corrected. New and not well-known; provides a feeling of natural light. More expensive.

When using incandescent lighting with fluorescent, select a deluxe warm white or soft white fluorescent. Avoid daylight white fluorescents altogether. If the home buyer selects the colors for the bathroom or if you're decorating a model, consult the above chart for choosing the fluorescent lighting. By choosing the type of fluorescent light that enhances the color, you will create an inviting room that flatters the occupants.

The wattage of fluorescent lights is directly proportional to tube length. The wattage required should be decided in the planning stages, because you cannot switch a 20-watt tube for a 40-watt one.

The amount of either fluorescent or incandescent general lighting recommended by the National Kitchen and Bath Association is as follows:

Fluorescent lights—1.2 watts to 1.6 watts per square foot
Incandescent lights—3½ watts to 4 watts per square foot
Luminous ceilings—3.3 watts per square foot

The minimum standards for lighting distilled from the recommendations for baths by the American Home Lighting Institute and General Electric Company are discussed in the following paragraphs.

If using a ceiling light with a small mirror (less than 36 inches wide), the light should be aligned with the front edge of the sink or counter. Sidelights around the mirror should be centered 60 inches above the floor, 30 inches apart.

If using fluorescent lights, use two 24-inch, 20-watt tubes on each side of the mirror, connected to wall brackets. A fluorescent ceiling fixture should consist of two 24-inch, 20-watt tubes or a combination of a 22-watt and 32-watt circline ceiling fixture.

If using incandescent lighting, install two wall brackets or hanging fixtures with a minimum diameter of 6 inches to accommodate one 75-watt or two 40- to 60-watt soft white bulbs in each. A ceiling fixture should accommodate 100 to 120 watts and have a minimum diameter of 12 inches.

If you want to illuminate a large mirror (36 inches or wider) with fluorescent lighting, install two 36-inch or 48-inch tubes in a diffusing fixture over the mirror or a double row of 36-inch, 30-watt or 48-inch, 40-watt tubes recessed in the ceiling or surface mounted and placed over the front edge of the counter. The preferred method is recessing the lighting in a soffit that is 18 to 24 inches wide; the fixture should extend the length of the counter and at least 8 inches from the ceiling. The bottom of the soffit should be placed 78 inches above the floor. Incandescent lighting for this size of mirror should consist of three or four 60-watt bulbs in separate diffusers extending at least 22 inches across the top of the mirror. A light fixture should extend the entire length of an extremely large mirror or at least within a foot of entire mirror length.

If using the theatrical style of lighting, it should consist of at least six exposed white globe bulbs per strip across the top and down each side. Strips should be placed 30 inches apart and never mounted on the ceiling. To prevent glare, use 15- to 25-watt bulbs.

In separate compartments for a toilet and bidet or other fixtures, use a fluorescent ceiling fixture with a minimum diameter of 8 inches with a 22-watt or 32-watt circline unit. If using a wall bracket, use one 36-inch, 30-watt tube. Or use an incandescent wall or ceiling fixture at least 8 inches wide with a 75-watt bulb.

If local codes permit, use a recessed vapor-proof fixture with a 60- or 75-watt bulb when illuminating an enclosed shower or tub. Position the switch out of reach of someone inside the enclosure.

Provide light good enough for reading for tubs that are not enclosed. Fixtures should be vapor proof.

Lighting in a powder room need not be as bright as in other baths, since these are not used for shaving or make-up application, in general. A mirror less than 36 inches wide should be surrounded by two wall fixtures, 30 inches apart and 60 inches above the floor, with two 75-

watt bulbs or 20-watt tubes. A fixture that is wall mounted over a mirror should be at least 10 inches long, with two 75-watt or four 40-watt bulbs or two 18-inch, 15-watt or 24-inch, 20-watt fluorescent tubes. Place soffit-mounted lights 78 inches above the floor.

Electrical shocks are a prime cause of bathroom accidents. The National Electrical Code (NEC) requires that switches and receptacles in rooms with high humidity, water, and electricity be located out of reach of someone in a tub or shower. Receptacles must be GFCI types or controlled by a GFC breaker.

The GFCI receptacle is designed to sense a short circuit within an instant, which prevents electrocution. It should have a reset switch built in.

The GFC breaker is installed in the service panel. It makes sense to put all lines to baths on a GFC breaker, not just those servicing the tub and shower areas. Of course, the room must be properly ventilated to prevent excessive steam or humidity from tripping the breaker.

Ventilating the Bathroom

To determine the minimum fan rating necessary for a bathroom, multiply the length and width of the room by 1.1 (in a room with an 8-foot ceiling); thus, a 6-foot × 8-foot room would use this formula:

$$6 \times 8 \times 1.1 = 52.8 \text{ CFM (which rounds off to 53 CFM)}$$

One sone is equivalent to the sound of a quiet refrigerator in a quiet room. The recommended sone level for fans is as close to 1.5 sones as possible. The National Kitchen and Bath Association holds that 6.5 sones is the maximum permissible noise level for fans (Home Ventilating Institute 1980).

Exhaust fans require ducts exhausted to the exterior. Ducts should be in straight runs for free airflow. In spite of dampers, the possibility of a back-draft exists in cold weather, so place openings so that cold air will not hit a bather.

Insulating the Bathroom

The recognized method for rating the performance of sound-isolating construction is based on the Sound Transmission Class or STC (U.S. Savings and Loan League 1970). In general, if the sound transmission between rooms is reduced to the point where conversation cannot be understood in an adjoining room, then an acceptable level of privacy has been achieved. The FHA-acceptable STC ratings for multifamily dwellings serve as a guide in judging all houses for sound isolation.

Noises caused by tubs, showers, and toilets, and heating and ventilating equipment, as well as appliances, also must be controlled.

Single gypsum board walls have a poor resistance to sound transmission, generally resulting in an STC of about 34. Insulation within the stud cavities does not increase the sound isolation appreciably. The weight of the gypsum board must be doubled, or the two wall surfaces must be mechanically separated to achieve an STC rating of more than 40.

Increasing the weight of the construction and/or using "discontinuous" construction methods plus adding sound-absorbing materials in the walls help reduce these noises.

Adding insulation to a resiliently mounted wall increases the acoustical

Figure 73. Sound-deadening board

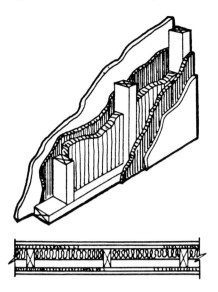

performance in proportion to the thickness of the insulation and can reduce sound level as much as 10 decibels (dB). Noise isolation performance depends on surfacing materials and how they are installed. Backer strips for attaching baseboards or horizontal blocking at the top and middle height for fire prevention decrease the performance. Resilient channels must be handled and installed carefully to avoid permanent deflection.

To obtain an STC of 50 or more, without regard for fire ratings, channels must be used throughout, in place of gypsum backing strips, to totally float the surfacing materials and resilient caulking used on all edges.

Sound-deadening board applied to both sides of a single-stud wall (Figure 73) provides resilient mounting, if the surfacing materials are correctly laminated to the board; this can result in a wall with an STC rating of approximately 46. If the surfacing materials are nailed to meet fire-rating requirements, however, the STC is reduced to the following: 10 dB with 8 inches on center, 8 dB with 16 inches on center, and 4 dB with 24 inches on center.

Staggered wall studs (Figure 74) with one layer of gypsum board on each side on 2-inch × 4-inch studs with a single 2-inch × 6-inch plate produce an STC of approximately 42. Adding insulation in the stud cavity or sound-deadening board to each side increases this to 45-49 STC.

Cabinets can be mounted on staggered stud construction without reducing its acoustical effectiveness.

Double stud walls (see Figure 75) increase the STC by about 9 dB. Walls are 2-inch × 4-inch stud walls on two separate 2-inch × 3-inch or 4-inch plates spaced ¼-1 inch apart. Adding insulation raises the STC as high as 59. Sound-deadening board yields about a 50 STC.

Surface cabinets mounted on double stud walls do not reduce acoustical effectiveness. The separate walls should not be tied together with plumbing or wiring.

Where walls and floors are joined, take precautions to prevent airborne and structure-borne sounds.

To prevent airborne sounds, the floor/ceiling system should be comparable to the wall system. Spaces between floor joists should be blocked at the juncture of walls and floors to reduce sound.

Discontinuous construction should be used between the structural floor and the finished ceiling by resilient mounting of the ceiling or use of separate ceiling joists. Insulation can be included in the cavities between the discontinuous frame and works with a resiliently mounted ceiling. A floating floor construction that resiliently floats the finished floor from the subfloor and/or structural floor also helps isolate sound.

Wall systems that isolate sound require proper installation of surfacing material, which should be installed over the entire wall area, behind tubs, soffits, cabinets, and duct enclosures, where structural framing might otherwise be left exposed. Resilient, nonhardening caulking must be used at floor and ceiling of all partitions and around all perforations, such as electrical outlets, plumbing, and other openings (Figure 76).

Figure 74. Staggered stud walls

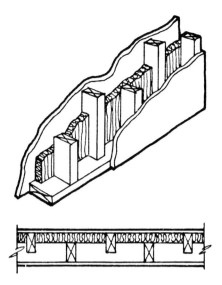

Figure 75. Double stud walls

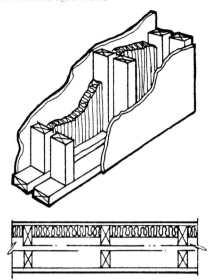

Figure 76. Resilient caulking around plumbing

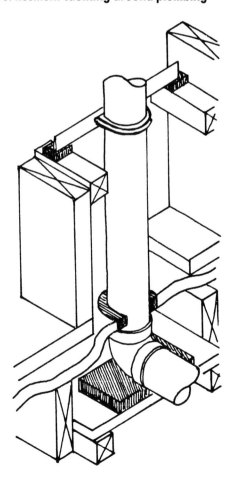

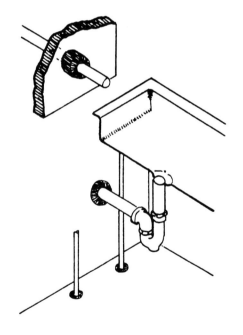

Appendix 4

Templates and Graph Paper

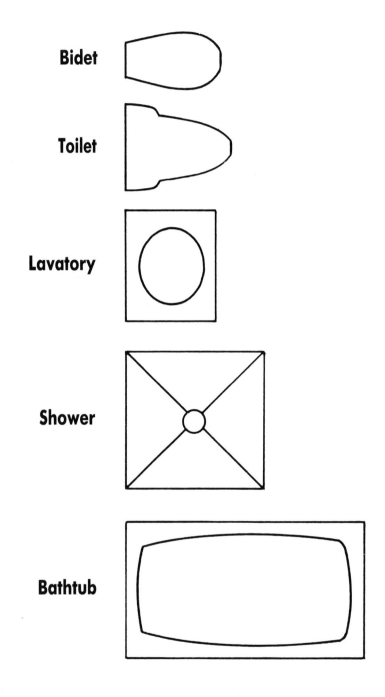

Bidet

Toilet

Lavatory

Shower

Bathtub

Common Architectural Graphic Symbols

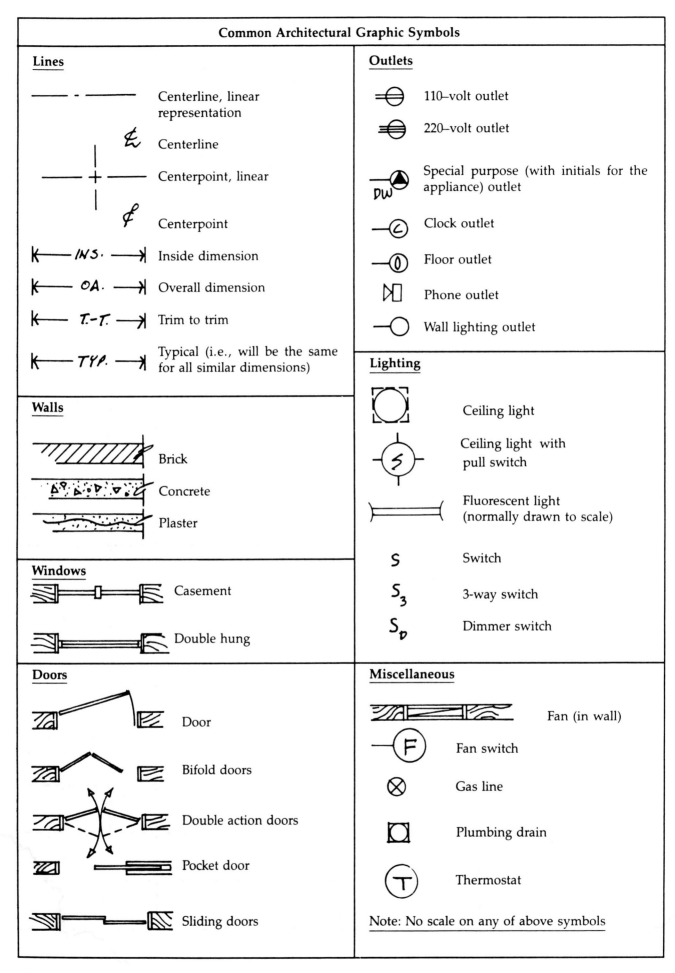

Lines

——— - ——— Centerline, linear representation

℄ Centerline

———+——— Centerpoint, linear

₵ Centerpoint

|←— INS. —→| Inside dimension

|←— OA. —→| Overall dimension

|←— T.-T. —→| Trim to trim

|←— TYP. —→| Typical (i.e., will be the same for all similar dimensions)

Walls

Brick

Concrete

Plaster

Windows

Casement

Double hung

Doors

Door

Bifold doors

Double action doors

Pocket door

Sliding doors

Outlets

110–volt outlet

220–volt outlet

DW Special purpose (with initials for the appliance) outlet

Clock outlet

Floor outlet

Phone outlet

Wall lighting outlet

Lighting

Ceiling light

Ceiling light with pull switch

Fluorescent light (normally drawn to scale)

S Switch

S_3 3-way switch

S_D Dimmer switch

Miscellaneous

Fan (in wall)

F Fan switch

Gas line

Plumbing drain

T Thermostat

Note: No scale on any of above symbols

References

American Association of Retired Persons. *A Profile of Older Americans.* Washington, DC: AARP, 1985.

American Home Lighting Institute. *Lighting Guidelines.* Chicago, IL: AHLI, 1985.

American National Standards Institute. *American National Standard for Buildings and Facilities—Providing Accessibility and Usability for Physically Handicapped People.* New York, NY: ANSI, 1986.

Arnold, Don. *College of Product Knowledge.* Skokie, IL: Supply House Times, Plumbing and Heating Publishing Company, 1979.

Cheever, Ellen. *The Basics of Bathroom Design . . . and Beyond.* Hackettstown, NJ: National Kitchen and Bath Association, 1985.

"Consumer Bathroom Remodeling Report." *Kitchen and Bath Business.* 31 (November 1985): 53-76.

Fletcher, June and Woodcock, Deborah. "Ninth Annual Home Buyer Survey," *Builder* 9 (July 1986): 72-90.

Home Ventilating Institute. *Home Ventilating Guide, Publication 12.* Rolling Meadows, IL: HVI, 1980.

Kira, Alexander. *The Bathroom.* New York, NY: Bantam Books, 1976.

Lazer, William. "Inside The Mature Market," *American Demographics* 7 (March 1985): 22.

Maass, James E. "A New Generation of Cultured Marble: Countertops, Solid Colors, An Array of Textures, Even Granite Looks," *Kitchen and Bath Business* 33 (May 1987): 166-169.

National Association of Home Builders. *Decisions for the '90s.* Washington, DC: NAHB, 1985.

———. *Housing Issues and Answers.* Washington, DC: NAHB, 1985.

"Nationwide Survey," *Kitchen and Bath Design News* 4 (October 1986): 52-55.

O'Connor, Dan. *Advanced Design Notes.* Kreamer, PA: Wood-Mode Cabinetry, 1986.

Platek, Russell W. *Bathroom Specialist Training Manual.* Hackettstown, NJ: National Kitchen and Bath Association, 1986.

Small Homes Council—Building Research Council. *Bathroom Planning Standards, C5.7.* Champaign, IL: SHC-BRC, 1979.

Television Digest, Inc. *TV Factbook.* Washington, DC, 1958.

The Conference Board, Consumer Research Center. *Baby Boomers in Mid-Passage.* New York, NY: CB,CRC, 1987.

"Thirteenth Annual Consumer/Builder Survey," *Professional Builder* 51 (December 1986): 90.

United States Savings and Loan League. *Construction Lending Guide.* Chicago, IL: USSLL, 1970.

U.S. Department of Commerce, Bureau of the Census. *1983 Annual Housing Survey.* Washington, DC: U.S. DOC, 1983.

———. *Plumbing Fixtures.* Washington, DC: U.S. DOC, 1986.

Wright, Lawrence. *Clean and Decent.* New York, NY: The Viking Press, 1960.